PREFACE.

One of the sacred writers of the olden time is reported to have said: "Of the making of many books, there is no end." This remark will, to a great extent, apply to the number of works published upon the all important subject of Cookery. The oft-repeated saying, attributed to old sailors, that the Lord sends victuals, and the opposite party, the cooks, is familiar to all.

Notwithstanding the great number and variety of so-called cookbooks extant, the author of this treatise on the culinary art, thoroughly impressed with the belief that there is ample room for one more of a thoroughly practical and every day life, common sense character—in every way adapted to the wants of the community at large, and looking especially to the preparation of healthful, palatable, appetizing and nourishing food, both plain and elaborately compounded—and in the preparation of which the very best, and, at the same time, the most economical material is made use of, has ventured to present this new candidate for the public approval. The preparation of this work embodies the result of more than thirty years personal and practical experience. The author taking nothing for granted, has thoroughly tested the value and entire correctness of every direction he has given in these pages. While carefully catering to the varied tastes of the mass, everything of an unhealthful, deleterious, or even doubtful character, has been carefully excluded; and all directions are given in the plainest style, so as to be readily understood, and fully comprehended by all classes of citizens.

The writer having been born and brought up on a farm, and being in his younger days of a delicate constitution, instead of joining in the rugged work of the field, remained at home to aid and assist his mother in the culinary labors of the household. It was in this home-school—in its way one of the best in the world, that he acquired not only a practical knowledge of what he desires to fully impart to others, but a taste for the preparation, in its most attractive forms, of every variety of palatable and health-giving food. It was his early training in this homely school that induced him to make this highly important matter an all-absorbing theme and the subject of his entire life study. His governing rule in this department has ever been the injunction laid down by the chief of the Apostles: "Try all things; prove all things; and hold fast that which is good."

INTRODUCTORY.

A Brief History of the Culinary Art, and its Principal Methods.

Cooking is defined to be the art of dressing, compounding and preparing food by the aid of heat. Ancient writers upon the subject are of opinion that the practice of this art followed immediately after the discovery of fire, and that it was at first an imitation of the natural processes of mastication and digestion. In proof of the antiquity of this art, mention is made of it in many places in sacred writ. Among these is notably the memoirs of the Children of Israel while journeying in the wilderness, and their hankering after the "flesh-pots of Egypt."

Among the most enlightened people of ancient times,—cooking, if not regarded as one of the fine arts, certainly stood in the foremost rank among the useful. It was a highly honored vocation, and many of the most eminent and illustrious characters of Greece and Rome did not disdain to practice it. Among the distinguished amateurs of the art, in these modern times, may be mentioned Alexander Dumas, who plumed himself more upon his ability to cook famous dishes than upon his world-wide celebrity as the author of the most popular novels of his day.

In the state in which man finds most of the substances used for food they are difficult of digestion. By the application of heat some of these are rendered more palatable and more easily digested, and, consequently, that assimilation so necessary to the sustenance of life, and the repair of the constant waste attendant upon the economy of the human system. The application of heat to animal and vegetable substances, for the attainment of this end, constitutes the basis of the science of cookery.

BROILING, which was most probably the mode first resorted to in the early practice of this art, being one of the most common of its various operations, is quite simple and efficacious. It is especially adapted to the wants of invalids, and persons of delicate appetites. Its effect is to coagulate, in the quickest manner, upon the surface the albumen of the meat, effectually sealing up its pores, and thus retaining the rich juices and delicate flavor that would otherwise escape and be lost.

ROASTING comes next in order, and for this two conditions are essentially requisite—a good, brisk fire, and constant basting. As in the case of broiling, care should be taken at the commencement to coagulate the albumen on the surface as speedily as possible. Next to broiling and stewing, this is the most economical mode of cooking meats of all kinds.

BAKING meat is in very many respects objectionable—and should never be resorted to when other modes of cooking are available, as it reverses the order of good, wholesome cookery, in beginning with a slow and finishing with a high temperature. Meats cooked in this manner have never the delicate flavor of the roast, nor are they so easily digested.

BOILING is one of the easiest and simplest methods of cooking, but in its practice certain conditions must be carefully observed. The fire must be attended to, so as to properly regulate the heat. The utensils used for this purpose, which should be large enough to contain sufficient water to completely cover the meat, should be scrupulously clean, and provided with a close-fitting cover. All scum should be removed as fast as it rises, which will be facilitated by frequent additions of small quantities of cold water. Difference of opinion exists among cooks as to the propriety of putting meats in cold water, and gradually raising to the boiling point, or plunging into water already boiling. My own experience, unless in the preparation of soups, is decidedly in favor of the latter. Baron Liebig, the highest authority in such matters, decidedly favors this process. As in the case of roasting, the application of boiling water coagulates the albumen, thus retaining the juices of the meat that would be dissolved in the liquid.

STEWING is generally resorted to in the preparation of made dishes, and almost every variety of meats are adapted to this method. The better the quality of the meats, as a matter of course, the better the dish prepared in this way; but, by careful stewing, the coarser and rougher quality of meats can be rendered soft, tender and digestible, a desirable object not generally attained in other modes. Add pieces of meat, trimmings, scraps and bones, the latter containing a large amount of palatable and nourishing gelatine, may be thus utilized in the preparation of wholesome and appetizing dishes at a comparatively trifling cost.

An Explanatory Word in Conclusion.

As a matter of strict justice to all parties concerned, the author of this work deems it proper to explain his reasons for mentioning in the body of some of the recipes given in this book, the places at which the purest and best articles used are to be purchased. This recommendation is, in every instance, based upon a thorough and complete personal test of every article commended. In these degenerate days of wholesale adulteration of almost every article of food and drink, it is eminently just and proper that the public should be advised where the genuine is to be procured. Without desiring to convert his book into a mere advertising medium, the author deems it not out of place to give the names of those dealers in this city of whom such articles as are essential in the preparation of many of the recipes given in these pages may be procured—of the most reliable quality, and at reasonable rates.

SOUPS.

Stock.

The foundation—so to speak—and first great essential in compounding every variety of appetizing, and at the same time wholesome and nourishing soups, is the stock. In this department, as in some others, the French cooks have ever been pre-eminent. It was said of this class in the olden time that so constantly was the "stock"—as this foundation has always been termed—replenished by these cooks, that their rule was never to see the bottom of the soup kettle. It has long been a fixed fact that in order to have good soup you must first have good stock to begin with. To make this stock, take the liquor left after boiling fresh meat, bones, (large or small, cracking the larger ones in order to extract the marrow,) bones and meat left over from a roast or broil, and put either or all of these in a large pot or soup kettle, with water enough to cover. Let these simmer slowly—never allowing the water to boil—taking care, however, to keep the vessel covered—stirring frequently, and pouring in occasionally a cup of cold water, and skimming off the scum. It is only where fresh meat is used that cold water is applied at the commencement; for cooked meat, use warm. The bones dissolved in the slow simmering, furnish the gelatine so essential to good stock. One quart of water to a pound of meat is the average rule. Six to eight hours renders it fit for use. Let stand over night; skim off the fat; put in an earthen jar, and it is ready for use. Every family should keep a jar of the stock constantly on hand, as by doing so any kind of soup may be made from it in from ten to thirty minutes.

General Directions for Making Soup.

Having prepared your stock according to the foregoing directions, take a sufficient quantity, when soup is required, and season, as taste may dictate, with sweet and savory herbs—salpicant, celery salt, or any other favorite seasoning—adding vegetables cut fine, and let the same boil slowly in a covered vessel until thoroughly cooked. If preferred, after seasoning the stock, it may be thickened with either barley, rice, tapioca, sago, vermicelli, macaroni, farina or rice flour. A roast onion is sometimes added to give richness and flavor. It is a well-known fact that soups properly prepared improve in flavor and are really better on the day after than when first made. By substituting different materials, garnitures, flavorings and condiments, of which an endless variety is available, the intelligent housewife may be able to furnish a different soup for every day of the year. In following these, as in all other directions for every department of cookery, experience will, after all, be found the great teacher and most valuable aid and adjunct to the learner of the art.

Calves'-Head Soup.

Take a calf's head of medium size; wash clean, and soak it an hour or more in salted water; then soak a little while in fresh, and put to boil in cold water; add a little salt and a medium-sized onion; take off the scum as it rises, and as the water boils away add a little soup stock; when quite tender take the meat from the bone, keeping the brain by itself; strain the soup, and if you think there is too much meat, use a portion as a side-dish dressed with brain sauce; do not cut the meat too fine—and season the soup with allspice, cloves and mace, adding pepper and salt to taste; put back the meat, and taking one-half the brain, a lump of butter, and a spoonful of flour, work to a thin batter, stirring in claret and sherry wines to taste, and last of all add a little extract of lemon, and one hard-boiled egg, chopped not too fine; if desirable add a few small force-meat balls.

[Turtle soup may be made in the same manner.]

Ox-Tail Soup.

Take one ox-tail and divide into pieces an inch long; 2 pounds of lean beef cut in small pieces; 4 carrots; 3 onions sliced fine; a little thyme, with pepper and salt to taste, and 4 quarts cold water; boil four hours or more, according to size of the ox-tail, and when done add a little allspice or cloves.

Okra Soup.

One large slice of ham; 1 pound of beef, veal or chicken, and 1 onion, all cut in small pieces and fried in butter together until brown, adding black or red pepper for seasoning, along with a little salt, adding in the meantime, delicately sliced thin, sufficient okra, and put all in a porcelain kettle. For a family of four use 30 pods of okra, with 2 quarts water, over a steady, but not too hot fire; boil slowly for 3 or 4 hours; when half done add 2 or 3 peeled tomatoes.

Chicken Gumbo.

[Mrs. E. A. Wilburn's Recipe.]

For the stock, take two chickens and boil in a gallon of water until thoroughly done and the liquid reduced to half a gallon. Wipe off $1\frac{1}{2}$ pounds of green okra, or if the dry is used, $\frac{1}{2}$ pound is sufficient, which cut up fine and add to this stock while boiling; next add $1\frac{1}{2}$ pounds of ripe tomatoes, peeled and chopped fine, adding also $\frac{1}{2}$ coffee cupful of rice; let these boil for six hours, adding boiling water when necessary; then take out the chickens, carve and fry them brown in clear lard; into the fat put 1 large white onion, chopped fine, adding 2 tablespoonfuls of flour. Just before serving, put the chicken, boned and chopped, with the gravy thus prepared, and add to the soup with salt and pepper to taste.

Fresh Oyster Soup.

Take 25 or 30 small Eastern and 50 California oysters; wash clean, and put into a kettle over the fire, with a little over a pint of water. As soon as they open pour into a pan and take the oysters from the shells, pouring the juice into a pitcher to settle. If the oysters are large, cut in two once; return the juice to the fire, and when it boils put in a piece of butter worked in flour; season with pepper and salt, and let it boil slowly for two minutes; put in a cupful of rich milk and the oysters, along with a sufficient quantity of chopped crackers, and let the liquid boil up once. Should you need a larger quantity of soup, add a can of good oysters, as they will change the flavor but little. In my opinion nutmeg improves the flavor of the soup.

Fish Chowder.

Take 4 pounds of fresh codfish—the upper part of the fish is best; fry plenty of salt pork cut in small strips; put the fat in the bottom of the kettle, then a layer of the fried pork, next a layer of fish; follow with a layer of potato sliced—not too thin—and a layer of sliced onions, seasoned with plenty of salt and pepper; alternate these layers as long as the material holds out, topping off with a layer of hard crackers. Use equal parts of water and milk sufficient to cook, which will not require more than three-quarters of an hour, over a good fire. Great care should be taken not to scorch in the cooking.

[Clam Chowder may be made according to the foregoing formula, substituting 3 pints of clams for the fish.]

Clam Soup.

Take 50 small round clams; rinse clean, and put in a kettle with a pint of water; boil for a few minutes, or until the shells gape open; empty into a pan, pick the meat from the shells, and pour the juice into a pitcher to settle; chop the clams quite small; return the juice to the fire, and as soon as hot, work in a good-sized lump of butter, with a little flour, and juice of the clams; stir in a teacup of milk; season with black pepper, and after letting this boil for two minutes, put in the clams, adding at the same time chopped cracker or nudels, and before taking up, a little chopped parsley.

Clam Chowder.

One hundred small clams chopped fine; $\frac{1}{2}$ pound fat salt pork put in pot and fried out brown; 2 small or 1 large onion, and 1 tomato chopped fine. Put all in the pot with the clam juice and boil for two hours, after which add rolled crackers and 1 pint hot milk, letting it boil up. Season with salt and pepper, adding a little thyme if agreeable to taste.

Baked Beans and Bean Soup.

Take three pints of white peas or army beans; wash very clean; soak eight hours; rinse and put to boil with plenty of water, hot or cold, with $1\frac{1}{2}$ pounds beef soup-meat and $\frac{1}{2}$ pound of salt pork, letting these boil slowly, and skimming as the scum rises. Stir frequently, as the beans are apt to scorch when they begin to soften. When soft enough to be easily crushed with the thumb and finger, season with plenty of black pepper and salt; after five minutes have elapsed fill a nice baking pan—such a one as will do to set on the table—pour in the liquid until it nearly covers the beans, score the pork and put it half-way down in the beans, and bake in a slow fire until nicely browned.

When the remaining beans are boiled quite soft rub them through a colander into the soup; add 1 pint of milk, and season with ground cloves or mace. Just before taking up cut some toast the size of the end of a finger and add to the soup. Pepper sauce gives a nice flavor.

Dry Split-Pea Soup.

Soak one quart dry or split peas ten or twelve hours, and put on to boil in 1 gallon of water, with 1 pound soup-beef, and a small piece of the hock end of ham, nicely skinned and trimmed, (but if you do not have this at hand supply its place with a small piece of salt pork;) season with salt, pepper and a little ground cloves, adding a little curry or sweet marjoram; boil slowly until quite tender; rub the peas through a colander, adding a little rich milk. This soup should be rather thick. Cut bread in pieces the size of the little finger, fry in butter or lard, and put in the tureen when taken up.

Tomato Soup.

To one gallon good beef stock add $1\frac{1}{2}$ dozen ripe tomatoes, or 1 two-pound can; 2 carrots, 2 onions and 1 turnip cut fine; boil all together for an hour and a half, and run through a fine tin strainer; take a stewpan large enough to hold the liquid, and put it on the fire with $\frac{1}{2}$ pound of butter worked in two tablespoonfuls of flour; after mixing well together add a tablespoonful of white sugar; season with salt and pepper to taste, stirring well until the liquor boils, when skim and serve. The above quantity will provide sufficient for a large family.

Celery Soup.

To make good celery soup take 2 or 3 pounds of juicy beef—the round is best, being free from fat. Cover with cold water, and boil slowly for three or four hours. An hour before taking from the fire take 1 pound or more of celery, cut 4 or 5 inches long, taking also the root cut thin, and salting to taste, boil until quite tender; then take out the celery, dressing with pepper and salt or drawn butter. If you have some soup stock put in a little, boil a few minutes and strain. This is a most palatable soup, and the celery, acting as a sedative, is one of the best things that can be used for quieting the nerves.

Pepper-Pot.

Take thick, fat and tender tripe; wash thoroughly in water in which a little soda has been dissolved; rinse well, and cut in strips half the length of your little finger; after boiling ten minutes, put in a colander and rinse with a little hot water; then, adding good soup stock, boil until tender; season with cayenne pepper and salt, a little Worcestershire or Chutney sauce, and some small pieces of dough made as for nudels. Should the soup not be thick enough add a little paste of butter and flour; you may also add curry if you are fond of it.

This soup was popular in the Quaker City fifty years ago, and has never decreased in favor among the intelligent inhabitants.

Egg-Balls for Soup

Boil 3 eggs seven minutes, and mash the yolks with one raw egg, a tablespoonful of flour and a little milk; season with pepper, salt, and parsley or summer savory; make into balls and boil two or three minutes, and put in the soup just before serving. Excellent for both pea and bean soup.

Nudels.

Rich nudels undoubtedly form the best thickening for nice, delicate soups, such as chicken, veal, oyster and clam. Nudels are made with flour, milk and eggs, and a little salt, mixed to stiff dough, rolled as thin as possible, and cut in fine shreds the length of the little finger. In all soups where nudels are used, a little chopped parsley should be added just before taking up.

FISH.

FISH.

The so-termed food fishes are to be found without number in all portions of the world, civilized and savage, and a large portion of the inhabitants of the globe are dependant upon this source for their subsistence. Certain learned physiologists have put forth the theory that food-fish is brain-producing, and adds to the mental vigor of those who subsist upon it. While we are not disposed to controvert this consoling idea—if the theory be true—the South Sea savages, who live upon this aliment, both in the raw and cooked state—and the Esquimaux, whose principal summer and winter diet is frozen fish—should be the most intelligent people on earth.

The modes of preparing fish for the table are equally as numerous as the species. The direction given by Mrs. Glass, in a cook-book of the olden time, is at the same time the most original and most sensible. This lady commences with: "First catch your fish."

BOILED FISH.

Fresh fish should never lie in water. As soon as cleaned, rinse off, wipe dry, wrap carefully in a cotton cloth, and put into salted boiling water. If cooked in this manner the juice and flavor will be fully retained. Twenty minutes boiling will thoroughly cook a medium sized fish.

FRIED FISH.

In frying large-sized fish, cut the slices lengthwise instead of across, for if cut against the grain the rich juices will be lost in the cooking, rendering the fish hard, dry and tasteless. For this reason fish are always better cooked whole, when this can be done. Beat up one or two eggs, with two tablespoonfuls of milk, with salt to season. After dipping the fish in this, dry in cracker dust—never use corn meal—and fry in good lard.

Broiling Fish.

In broiling fish, cut large as in frying, grease the bars of the gridiron. Harden both sides slightly, and baste with butter, seasoning with pepper and salt.

Fried Oysters.

Take large oysters, drain the juice, and dry them with a cloth, and run them in eggs, well beaten with a little milk; season with pepper and a little salt, and after drying in cracker dust, fry in equal parts best lard and butter, until a light brown.

Oysters in Batter.

Save all the juice of the oysters; beat two eggs with two or three spoonfuls of milk or cream, seasoning with pepper; put this into the juice, with the addition of as much flour as will make a rich batter. When the fat is quite hot put into it a spoonful of the batter, containing one oyster, and turn quickly in order that both sides may be nicely done brown.

Oyster Patties.

Roll good puff-paste quite thin—and cut in round pieces $3\frac{1}{2}$ inches in diameter, on which put a rim of dough, about 1 inch or less high, which may be stuck on with a little beaten egg; next add a top-piece or covering, fitting loosely, and bake in this until a light brown, and put away until wanted. Stew oysters in their own juice, adding a little butter and cream; fill the patties with this, put on the lid, and set in the oven for five minutes, and send to the table. Can oysters, with a rich gravy, make an excellent patty prepared in this way.

Stewed Lobsters or Crabs.

Take a two-pound can of lobster, or two large crabs, and cut as for making salad, and season highly with prepared mustard, cayenne pepper, curry powder, or sauce piquant, and salt to taste. Put in a porcelain stewpan, with a little water, to prevent scorching, and, after letting it boil up once, add butter the size of an egg, and one tablespoonful of vinegar, or half a teacupful of white wine, and the juice of half a lemon, and the moment this boils add half a teacupful of cream or good milk, stirring at the same time. Set the stew aside, and heat up shortly before sending to the table. Putting slices of toast in the bottom of the dish before serving is a decided improvement.

Roast, Boiled, Baked, Broiled and Fried.

Retaining the Juices in Cooking Meats.

Too little attention is paid to one of the most important features of the culinary art—particularly in roasting, boiling, and broiling—that is the retention of the natural juices of various meats in cooking. Existing, as these always do, in a liquid form, unless this is carefully guarded against, these palatable and health-giving essences of all animal food, both tame and game, are apt to be wasted and dissipated in various forms, when the exercise of mature judgment and a little care would confine them to these meats in the course of preparation. By way of illustration, let us suppose that a fowl, a leg of mutton, or some of the many kinds of fish frequently served up in this way, is to be boiled in water. If put in cold water, and the heat gradually raised until it reaches the boiling point, the health-giving albumen—with the juices which give each its peculiar and pleasant flavor—are extracted from the meat and dissolved and retained in the water, rendering the flesh and fish insipid and in some cases almost tasteless. If, however, these are plunged at once into boiling water, thereby on the instant coagulating the albumen of the surface at least, and thereby closing the pores through which the inside albuminous juices would otherwise exude and be lost. Besides this albumen, there are other juices which are among the most important constituent parts of every variety of animal food in which are embodied much of its fine flavor and nutritive qualities, and deprived of which such food becomes unpalatable and tasteless. All meats, then, instead of being put into cold water, should at the start be plunged into boiling hot water, as this prevents the escape of these juices, and the retaining not only the delicate and fine flavor of the meat, but confining and retaining its nutritive qualities where they naturally and properly belong.

Roast Pig.

Take a sucking pig—one from three to five weeks old is best. When properly dressed lay in salted water for half an hour; take out and wipe dry inside and out; make a stuffing of bread and butter, mixing to a proper consistency with milk and a well beaten egg; season with salt, pepper and sage, with the addition of thyme or summer savory, and an onion chopped fine and stewed in butter with flour. Sew up, and roast for a long time in an oven not too hot, first putting a little water with lard or dripping in the pan. Baste frequently until done, taking care to keep the pan a little distance above the bottom of the range.

To Roast Turkeys and Chickens.

Turkeys and chickens for roasting should never be over a year old. After being properly cleaned, cut the wings at the first joint from the breast, pull the skin down the lower end of the neck, and cut off the bone. Cut the necks, wings and gizzards into small pieces suitable for giblet stew—which should be put on the fire before preparing the fowls for roasting—which should be done by cutting off the legs at the first joint from the feet. Make the stuffing of good bread, rubbed fine, with butter, pepper and salt, and a teaspoonful of baking powder, seasoning with thyme or summer savory, mixing to the consistency of dough, adding eggs, well beaten, with good milk or cream. Fill the breast, and tie over the neck-bone with strong twine, rubbing the sides of the fowl with a dry cloth, afterwards filling quite full. Sew up tight, tie up the legs, and encase the body with strong twine, wrapped around to hold the wings to the body. After rubbing well with salt and dredging lightly with flour, put the fowl in a pan, laying on top two or three thin slices of fat pork, salt or fresh. Put a little water in the pan, and baste frequently, but do not roast too rapidly; raise the pan at least two inches from the bottom of the range. All white meat should invariably be cooked well done, and turkey or chicken, to be eaten cold, should be wrapped while warm in paper or cloth. When prepared in this way they will always be found soft and tender when cooled.

When the giblets are stewed tender—which they must be in order to be good—chop a handful of the green leaves of celery, adding pepper and salt, and put in. Ten minutes before taking from the fire add a lump of butter worked in with a tablespoonful of flour and the yolk of two boiled eggs, letting simmer two or three minutes, then put in the whites of the eggs, chopped fine, with the addition of a little good milk or cream. Some of this stew, mixed with the drippings of the fowl, makes the best possible gravy.

Roasting Beef.

Never wash meat; simply wipe with a damp cloth, rub with salt and dredge with flour; put in the pan with a little of the suet chopped fine, and a teacupful of water; set in a hot oven, two inches above the bottom. The oven should be quite hot, in order to close the pores on the surface of the meat as quickly as possible. As the meat hardens reduce the heat a little, basting frequently. Turn two or three times during the roasting, taking care not to let the gravy scorch. Meat cooked in this way will be tender and juicy, and when done will be slightly red in the centre. Should it prove too rare, carve thin and lay in a hot pan with a little gravy for one minute. Beef will roast in from one and-half to two hours, according to size. All meats may be roasted in the same way, taking care in every case, that the albuminous juices do not escape.

A Good Way to Roast a Leg of Mutton.

Into a kettle, with hot water enough to cover, put a leg of mutton. Let it boil half an hour, and the moment it is taken from the water, salt, pepper, and dredge with flour, and put on to roast with one-half a teacup of water in the pan. Baste frequently, first adding a tablespoonful of lard. Cooked in this way the meat has none of the peculiar mutton flavor which is distasteful to many.

Clayton's Mode of Cooking Canvas-back Ducks.

That most delicately flavored wild fowl, the canvas-back duck, to be properly cooked, should be prepared in the following style:

The bird being properly dressed and cleaned, place in the opening, after drawing, a tablespoonful of salt dissolved in water—some add a stick of celery, or celery salt, to flavor, but this is not necessary. Sew up the opening with strong thread; have your fire in the grate red hot—that is, the oven almost red hot; place your duck therein, letting it remain nineteen minutes

—which will be amply sufficient time if your oven is at the proper heat—but as tastes differ in this as in other matters of cookery, some prefer a minute longer and others one less. Serve the duck as hot as possible, with an accompanying dish of hominy, boiled, of course; the only condiment to be desired is a little cayenne pepper; some prefer a squeeze of lemon on the duck; others currant jelly; but the simplest and most palatable serving is the directions given.

Clayton's Mode of Cooking California Quail, or Young Chickens.

Split the birds in the back, and wash, but do not let them remain in the water any time; dry with a cloth; salt and pepper well, and put in a pan with the inside up; also put in two or three slices of fresh or salt pork, and a piece of butter about the size of an egg, with three or four tablespoonfuls of water, and set the pan on the upper shelf of the range when quite hot, and commence basting frequently the moment the birds begin to harden on the top; and when slightly brown turn and serve the under side the same way, until that is also a little brown, taking care not to scorch the gravy. Having prepared a piece of buttered toast for each bird, lay the same in a hot dish, place the birds thereon, and pour the gravy over all. Birds cooked in this manner are always soft and juicy—whereas, if broiled, all the juices and gravy would have gone into the fire—and should you attempt cooking in that way, if not thoroughly, constantly basted, they are liable to burn; and if basted with butter it runs into the fire, smoking and destroying their rich natural flavor.

I have been thus particular in the directions detailed in this recipe, from the fact that many people have an idea that the quail of California are not equal to that of the Atlantic States, when, from my experience with both, which has been considerable, I find no difference in the flavor and juiciness of the birds when cooked in the way I have carefully laid down in the foregoing simple and easily understood directions.

To Cook Boned Turkey.

For the filling of the turkey, boil, skin, trim, and cut the size of the end of your finger, two fresh calves' tongues. At the same time boil for half-an-hour in soup stock, or very little water, a medium-sized, but not old, chicken; take all the meat from the bones, and cut as the calves' tongues. Take a piece of ham, composed of fat and lean, and cut small; also the livers of the turkey and the chicken, chopped fine, along with a small piece of veal, mostly fat, cut as the chicken, and half an onion chopped fine.

Put all these into a kettle with water to half cover, and stew until tender. At the time of putting on the fire, season with salt and pepper, ground mace, salpicant, celery salt and a little summer savory. Just before taking from the fire stir in the yolks of two eggs, well beaten, with three or four truffles chopped the size of a pea, and a teacupful of sherry or white wine. When this mixture is cold put it in the turkey, with the skin side out; draw it carefully around the filling, and sew up with a strong thread; and after wrapping it very tightly with strong twine, encase it in two or three thicknesses of cotton cloth, at the same time twisting the ends slightly. These precautions are necessary to prevent the escape of the fine flavor of this delicious preparation. Boil slowly for four hours or longer, in good soup stock, keeping the turkey covered with the liquid, and the vessel covered also. When taken up lay on a level surface, with a weight, to flatten the two sides a little, but not heavy enough to press out the juice. When quite cold take off the wrapping and thread, and lay on a nice large dish, garnishing with amber jelly cut the size of peas.

TO BONE A TURKEY.

Use a French boning knife, five inches in length and sharp at the point. Commence by cutting off the wings at the first joint from the breast; then the first joint from the drum-sticks, and the head, well down the neck. Next place the bird firmly on the table, with the breast down, and commence by cutting from the end of the neck, down the centre of the back, through to the bone, until you reach the Pope's nose. Then skin or peel the flesh as clean as possible from the frame, finishing at the lower end of the breast-bone.

Chickens may be boned in the same manner

To Cook Ducks or Chickens, Louisiana Style.

Carve the fowls at the joints, making three or four pieces of the breast; wash nicely in salted water, and put on to boil with water enough to cover, adding a little salt; boil slowly; carefully skimming off the scum. When the meat begins to get tender and the water well reduced, cook four onions, chopped fine, in a pan with pork fat and butter, dredging in a little flour and seasoning with pepper and salt, adding a little of the juice from the fowls. Next take up the pieces of the meat and roll in browned flour or cracker-dust, and fry slightly. If the butter is not scorched put in a little browned flour; stir in the onion, and put it back in the kettle with the meat of the fowl, simmering until the gravy thickens, and the meat is thoroughly tender.

Breast of Lamb and Chicken, Breaded.

Take the breast of lamb and one chicken—a year old is best—and after taking off the thin skin of the lamb, wash it well in cold salted water; then put on to boil, with sufficient cold slightly-salted water to cover it, and boil until tender—the addition of a medium-sized onion improves the flavor—then take up, and when quite cold, carve in nice pieces, and season with black pepper and salt. Next, beat two eggs, with two or three spoonfuls of milk or cream, and a spoonful of flour. After running the meat through this, roll in cracker-dust or browned flour, and fry in sweet lard and a little butter until a light brown. Next make a cream gravy; take a little of the liquid from the chicken, and make a rich thick drawn butter, and thinning it with cream, pour over the chicken while it is hot.

[The liquid used in boiling the chicken will make any kind of rich soup for dinner.]

Scrapple, or Haggis Loaf.

Take three or four pounds best fresh pork, mostly lean, with plenty of bones—the latter making a rich liquid. Put these into a kettle, and cover with hot or cold water, and let the mass boil slowly for two or three hours, or until quite tender, carefully removing the scum as it rises, after which take the meat out into a wooden bowl or tray. Pick out the bones carefully, and strain the liquid. After letting these stand for a few minutes, if in your opinion there is too much fat, remove a portion, and then return the liquor to the kettle, adding pepper and salt, and seasoning highly with summer savory. Next stir in two parts fine white corn-meal and one part buckwheat flour (Deming & Palmer's), until the whole forms quite a thick mush, after which, chopping the meat the size of the end of the finger, stir thoroughly into the mush. Next put the mixture into baking pans to the depth of $1\frac{1}{2}$ or 2 inches, and bake in a slow oven for two hours, or until the top assumes a light brown—taking care not to bake too hard on the bottom. Put in a cool place, and the next morning—when, after warming the pan slightly—so that the scrapple may be easily taken out—cut in slices of half-an-inch thick, which heat in a pan to prevent sticking, and serve hot.

[A small hog's head or veal is equally good for the preparation of this dish, which will be found a fine relish.]

Pigs' Feet and Hocks.

Have the feet nicely cleaned, and soaked for five or six hours, or over night, in slightly salted water. Boil until tender, and the large bones slip out easily, which will take from three to four hours. Take up, pull out the large bones, and lay in a stone jar, sprinkling on each layer a little salt and pepper, with a few cloves or allspice. After skimming off the fat, take equal parts of the water in which the feet were boiled, and good vinegar, and cover the meat in the jar.

This nice relish was known as "souse" fifty or sixty years ago, and is good, both cold or hot, or cut in slices and fried in butter for breakfast.

To Cook a Steak California Style of 1849-'50.

Cut a good steak an inch and an eighth thick. Heat a griddle quite hot, and rub over with a piece of the fat from the steak, after which lay on the steak for two or three minutes, or long enough to harden the under side of the steak, after which turn the other side, treating in the same way, thus preventing all escape of the rich juices of the meat. After this, cut a small portion of the fat into small and thin pieces, to which add sufficient butter to form a rich gravy, seasoning with pepper and salt to taste. A steak cooked in this way fully equals broiling, and is at the same time quite as juicy and tender.

A Good Way to Cook a Ham.

Boil a ten or twelve pound ham slowly for three hours; strip off the skin; take a sharp knife and shave off the outer surface very thin, and if quite fat take off a little, and spread over the fat part a thin coating of sugar. Next put the ham in a baking-pan, with one-half pint of white wine, and roast half-an-hour. Baste often, taking care that the wine and juice of the ham do not scorch, as these form a nice gravy. Whether eaten hot or cold the ham should be carved very thin.

Beefsteak Broiled.

Place the gridiron over a clear fire; rub the bars with a little of the fat, to keep from sticking. The moment it hardens a little—which closes the pores of the meat—turn it over, thus hardening both sides. You may then moisten with butter, or a little of the fat of the steak, and season with salt and pepper. Lay on a hot dish along with the best butter, which, with the juices of the meat, makes the best of gravy, and cooked in this style you have a most delicious steak.

Beefsteak with Onions.

Take five or six onions; cut fine, and put them in a frying-pan, with a small cup of hot water, and two ounces best butter, pepper and salt; dredge in a little flour, and let it stew until the onions are quite soft. Next broil the steak carefully. Lay on a hot dish, and lay the onions around, and not on top, of the steak, as that will create a steam, which will wilt and toughen it. To be eaten quite hot.

Corned Beef, and How to Cook It.

Select a piece of corned beef that is fat. The plate or navel pieces are best, and should only have been in salt five days. Put the piece in boiling water in a pot just large enough to hold it, along with an onion and a spoonful of cloves or allspice; let it boil slowly, skimming the first half hour, if to be eaten cold. Take it up as soon as tender, and when cool enough take out the bones and place the meat in a vessel just large enough to hold it, and pour in the fat, with sufficient hot water to cover it, letting it remain until quite cold.

[Beef tongues should be cooked in the same way, after laying in salt or strong pickle from twenty-four to thirty-six hours.]

Spiced Veal.

Take three pounds lean veal, parboiled, and one-fourth pound salt pork, each chopped fine; six soft crackers pounded; two eggs beaten; two teaspoonfuls of salt, three peppers, one nutmeg and a little thyme or summer savory. Mould up like bread, and place in a pan, leaving a space all around, in which place some of the water in which the meat was boiled. Bake until quite brown, and slice when cold.

Calves' Liver with Bacon.

Cut both liver and bacon in thin slices, and an inch long, taking off the skin. Place alternately on a skewer, and broil or roast in a quick oven. Dress with melted butter, pepper and juice of lemon.

Calves' or Lambs' Liver Fried.

Slice the liver thin, and season with salt and pepper. Beat an egg with a spoonful of milk or cream. Coat the slices with this, and dry in fine cracker dust. Fry in two parts lard and one of butter until a light brown. If fried too much the liver will be hard and tasteless. Salt pork fried brown is very nice with liver, and the fat from the pork will be found excellent to fry the liver in.

Spiced Beef.

Take 3½ pounds lean beef chopped small; six soda crackers rolled fine; 3 eggs well beaten; 4 tablespoonfuls sweet cream; butter size of an egg; 1½ tablespoonfuls salt, and one of pepper. Mix thoroughly, make into a loaf, and bake two hours, basting as you would roast beef.

FRIED OYSTERS.

Take the largest-sized oysters; drain off the juice, and dry in a cloth; beat two eggs in a spoonful of milk, adding a little salt and pepper. Run the oysters through this, and fry in equal parts butter and sweet lard to a light brown.

STEWS, SALADS and SALAD DRESSING.

Terrapin Stew.

Take six terrapins of uniform size. (The females, which are the best, may be distinguished by the lower shell being level or slightly projecting.) If the terrapins are large, use one pound of the best butter; if small, less, and a pint of good sherry wine. After washing the terrapins in warm water, put them in the kettle alive, and cover with cold water, keeping the vessel covered tight. After letting them boil until the shell cracks and you can crush the claws with the thumb and finger, take them off the fire, and when cool enough, pull off the shell and remove the dark, or scarf skin, next pulling the meat from the trail and the liver—being careful not to break the gall, which would render the liver uneatable. After breaking the meat in small pieces, lay it in a porcelain kettle with a teacupful of water; put in the wine, and one-half the butter, with 2 or 3 blades of mace, 2 or 3 teaspoonfuls of extract of lemon, 2 tablespoonfuls of Worcestershire or Challenge sauce; little salt is required, and if pepper is needed, use cayenne. After stewing for fifteen minutes, add the yolks of 6 hard-boiled eggs—worked to a paste in the remainder of the butter—thinning with the juice of the stew, adding at the same time a teacupful of sweet cream, and after simmering for three minutes, chop the whites of the eggs fine, and add to the mixture; then take from the fire, and make hot five minutes before serving. If kept in a cool place this stew will remain perfectly good for three days.

Stewed Chicken, Cottage Style, with White Gravy.

Take two chickens, one or two years old, and cut each in about fourteen pieces, dividing each joint, and cutting the breast in two pieces; cut the gizzard quite small, and put it and the liver with the chicken. When the chicken is half done, cover with cold water, adding a good-sized onion, and when it reaches a boil, skim carefully; and when the same is about half cooked add sufficient salt and pepper, and also a handful of the green leaves of celery chopped fine, which will give it the flavor of oysters. Boil slowly until you can tear the chicken with a fork, when turn it out in a dish. Next, take one half pound of good butter, the yolks of three boiled eggs, and two tablespoonfuls of corn-starch or flour, and, after working well together, so as to form a thin batter, add the liquor from the chicken, return to the kettle, and, after boiling for five minutes, return the chicken, season with nutmeg or sal-piquant, adding at the same time a teacupful of cream or good milk, also the whites of the eggs, chopped fine. Keep hot until served.

Stewed Tripe.

Cut and prepare the tripe as for pepper-pot; season highly; add a pint of soup stock, and four spoonfuls of tomatoes, with a little butter, and half an onion chopped fine. Cook until quite tender.

Chicken Salad.

Boil a good-sized chicken, not less than one year old, in as little water as possible; if you have two calves' feet boil them at the same time, salting slightly, and leaving them in after the chicken is cooked, that they may boil to shreds. This liquid forms a jelly, which is almost indispensable in making good salad. When the chicken becomes cold, remove the skin and bones, after which chop or cut to the size of a pea; cut celery and lettuce equally fine—after taking off the outer fibre of the former—and mixing, add Clayton's Salad Dressing, (the recipe for which will be found elsewhere); also incorporating four eggs, which should be boiled eight minutes, cutting three as fine as the chicken and celery, and leaving the fourth as a garnish on serving. Cold roast turkey, chicken or tender veal make most excellent salad treated in this way.

Clayton's Celebrated California Salad Dressing.

Take a large bowl, resembling in size and shape an ordinary wash-bowl, and a wooden spoon, fitted as nearly as possible to fit the curve of the bowl. First put in two or three tablespoonfuls of mixed mustard, quite stiff. Pour on this, slowly, one-fourth of a pint of best olive oil, stirring rapidly until thick; then break in two or three fresh eggs, and, after mixing slightly, pour in, very slowly, the remaining three-fourths of the pint of oil, stirring rapidly all the while until the mixture forms a thick batter. Next, take a teacupful of the best wine vinegar, to which the juice of one lemon has been added, along with a small tablespoonful of salt, and another of white sugar, stirring well, until the whole of these ingredients are thoroughly incorporated. When bottled and tightly corked, this mixture will remain good for months. Those who are not fond of the oil, will find that sweet cream, of about sixty or seventy degrees in temperature, a good substitute; but this mixture does not keep so well.

Salad Flavoring.

It will be found a good thing before ornamenting a salad, to take a section of garlic, and, after cutting off the end, steeping it in salt, and then rubbing the surface of the bowl, putting in at the same time, small pieces of the crust of French or other bread, similarly treated. Cover the bowl with a plate, and shake well. This gives the salad a rich, nutty flavor.

Eggs and Omelettes.

Boiling Eggs.

Unless quite sure the eggs are fresh, never boil them, as the well known remark that even to suspect an egg cooked in this style is undoubtedly well-founded. Hard boiled eggs, to be eaten either hot or cold, must never be boiled more than eight minutes, when they will be found tender and of a fine flavor, whereas, if boiled for a longer time, they will invariably prove leathery, tough, and almost tasteless, and dark-colored where the whites and yolk are joined, giving them an unsightly and anything but attractive appearance.

For soft boiled, three, and for medium, four minutes only, are necessary.

Scrambled Eggs.

Beat well three eggs, with two tablespoonfuls of cream or milk; add salt and pepper; put in the pan a lump of fresh butter, and, as soon as melted, put in the eggs, stirring rapidly from the time they begin to set; as in order to be tender they must be cooked quickly.

To Fry Eggs.

Put butter or lard in a hot pan, and then as many small, deep muffin rings as eggs required. Drop the eggs in the rings. Cooked in this manner the eggs are less liable to burn, look far nicer, and preserve their fine flavor.

Oyster Omelette.

Stew a few oysters in a little butter, adding pepper for seasoning, and when the omelette is cooked on the under side, put on the oysters, roll over, and turn carefully. A good omelette may be made of canned oysters treated in this way.

Ham Omelette.

Take a thin slice of the best ham—fat and lean—fry well done, and chop fine. When the omelette is prepared, stir in the ham, and cook to a light brown.

Cream Omelette.

Beat three eggs with two tablespoonfuls of cream, adding a little salt and pepper. Put a lump of butter in the pan, but do not let it get too hot before putting in the mixture. The pan should be about the temperature for baking batter cakes. Fold and turn over quite soon. The omelette should be a light brown, and be sent to the table hot. Should you have sausage for breakfast, the bright gravy from the sausage is preferable to butter in preparing the omelette.

Spanish Omelette.

Make in the same manner as the cream omelette, but before putting in the pan have ready one-half an onion, chopped fine and fried brown, with a little pepper and salt. When the omelette is cooked on one side, put the mixture on, and turn the sides over until closed tight.

Omelette for Dessert.

Beat eight eggs thoroughly, with a teacup of rich milk or cream, a tablespoonful of fine white sugar, and a very little salt. Stir well, and make in two omelettes; lay side by side, and sift over a thin coating of fine white sugar. In serving, pour over and around the omelette a wine-glass of good California brandy, and set on fire.

VEGETABLES.

BAKED TOMATOES.

Pick out large, fair tomatoes; cut a slice from the stem end, and, placing them in a pan with the cut side up, put into each one-half teaspoonful of melted butter, sprinkle with salt and pepper, and bake until they shrivel slightly.

RAW TOMATOES.

Cut the skin from both ends; slice moderately thin, and, if you like, add a small piece of onion chopped fine. Season with salt and pepper, and pour over Durkee's or Clayton's salad dressing.

CUCUMBERS.

Take off a thick rind, as that portion between the seed and outer skin is the unwholesome part. Slice, rather thin, into cold, salt water, and, after half-an-hour, drain off, and dress with salt, pepper, wine vinegar, and a little Chile pepper-sauce, covering slightly with Durkee's or Clayton's salad dressing.

BOILED CABBAGE.

Cut large cabbage in four; small in two pieces, and tie up in a bag or cloth. Put in boiling water, with some salt, and boil briskly for half-an-hour. A piece of charcoal in the pot will neutralize the odor given out by the cabbage, boiled in the ordinary way. Cabbage should never be cooked with corned-beef, as the fine flavor of the latter is changed to the strong odor of the cabbage.

TO COOK CAULIFLOWER.

If the cauliflower is large, divide in three, if small, in two pieces; tie up in a cloth, and put in boiling water with a little salt, and cook not more than twenty minutes. Eat with melted butter, pepper and salt, or nice drawn butter.

(Asparagus may be cooked in the same way, and eaten with similar dressing. Both cauliflower and asparagus may be spoiled with too much cooking. Care should be taken to drain the water from both as soon as they are done.)

To Cook Young Green Peas.

The best mode of cooking this most delicate and finely-flavored vegetable—put the peas in a porcelain-lined kettle, with just water sufficient to cover, and let them boil slowly until tender. Add a lump of butter, worked in a teaspoonful of flour, to the rich liquid, with half a teacupful of rich milk or cream; season with salt and pepper.

A Good Way to Cook Beets.

Take beets of a uniform size; boil until tender; slip off the skin, and slice into a dish or pan; season with salt and pepper, adding a little butter, made hot, and the juice of one lemon. Pour this over the beets, set in a hot oven for a few minutes, and send to the table hot.

Mashed Potatoes and Turnips.

Take equal quantities of boiled potatoes and turnips; mash together, adding butter, salt and pepper, and mix thoroughly with a little good milk, working all together until quite smooth.

Boiled Onions.

Take small white onions, if you have them; if large, cut and boil until tender, in salted water. Pour off nearly all the water, and add a small lump of butter, worked in a little flour, and a small cup of milk; add pepper, and simmer for a few minutes.

[All the foregoing are desirable additions to roast turkey and chicken.]

Stewed Corn.

If canned corn is used, put a sufficient quantity in a stewpan, with two or three spoonfuls of hot water, and, after adding pepper and salt to taste, put in a good-sized lump of butter, into which a teaspoonful of flour has been well worked, adding, at the same time, a cup of good, sweet milk or rich cream, and let it cook three minutes. Corn cut fresh from the cob should be boiled at least twenty minutes before adding the milk and butter.

Stewed Corn and Tomatoes.

Take equal quantities of corn and tomatoes, and stew together half-an-hour, with butter, pepper and salt; and when taken up place slices of buttered toast in the dish in which it is served.

Succotash.

This is the original native American Indian name for corn and beans. In compounding this most palatable and wholesome dish, take two or three pounds of green, climbing, or pole beans—the pods of which are large, and, at the same time, tender. Break these in pieces of something like half-an-inch long, and let them lie in cold water about half-an-hour, at which time drain this off. Put them in a porcelain-lined kettle, covering them with boiling water, into which put a large tablespoonful of salt. When the beans become tender, pour off the greater portion of the water, replacing it with that which is boiling, and when the beans become entirely tender, cut from the cob about half the amount of corn you have of the beans, which boil for twenty minutes; but where canned corn is used five minutes will suffice. About five minutes before taking from the fire, take a piece of butter about the size of an egg, worked with sufficient flour or corn-starch to form a stiff paste. Season with plenty of black pepper and salt to taste, adding, at the same time, a teacupful of rich milk or cream. Then, to keep warm, set back from the fire, not allowing to boil, but simmering slowly. This will be equally good the next day, if kept in a cool place, with an open cover, which prevents all danger of souring. This is a simple, healthful, and most appetizing dish, inexpensive and at the same time easily prepared.

Saratoga Fried Potatoes.

The mode of preparing the world-renowned Saratoga fried potatoes is no longer a secret. It is as follows:

Peel eight good-sized potatoes; slice very thin; use slicing-machine, when available, as this makes the pieces of uniform thickness. Let them remain half-an-hour in a quart of cold water, in which a tablespoonful of salt has been dissolved, and lay in a sieve to drain, after which mop them over with a dry cloth. Put a pound of lard in a spider or stewpan, and when this is almost, but not quite, smoking hot, put in the potatoes, stirring constantly to prevent the slices from adhering, and when they become a light brown, dip out with a strainer ladle.

[If preferred, cut the potatoes in bits an inch in length, and of the same width, treating as above.]

Salsify or Oyster Plant.

The best way I have yet found to cook this finely flavored and highly delicious vegetable is: First, wash clean, but do not remove the skin. Put the roots in more than enough boiling water to cover them; boil until quite soft; remove the skin; mash; add butter, and season with pepper and salt; make into the size of oysters, and dip in thin egg batter; fry a light brown. If the plant is first put into cold water to boil, and the skin scraped or removed, the delicate flavor of the oyster—which constitutes its chief merit—will be entirely dissipated and lost.

Egg Plant.

There is no more delicate and finely-flavored esculent to be found in our markets than the egg plant, when cooked in the right manner. Properly prepared, it is a most toothsome dish; if badly cooked, it is anything but attractive. Of all the varieties, the long purple is decidedly the best. Cut in slices, less than one-fourth an inch in thickness; sprinkle with salt, and let the slices lie in a colander half-an-hour or longer, to drain. Next parboil for a few minutes, and drain off the water; season with salt and pepper, and dip in egg batter, or beaten egg, and fry in sweet lard mixed with a little butter, until the slices are a light brown. Serve hot.

To Boil Green Corn.

Green corn should be put in hot water, with a handful of salt, and boiled slowly for half-an-hour, or five minutes longer. The minute the corn is done, pour off the water and let it remain hot. All vegetables are injured by allowing them to remain in the water after they are cooked.

Boiled Rice.

American rice for all its preparations is decidedly preferable, the grain being much the largest and most nutritious. In boiling, use two measures of water to one of rice, and let them boil until the water is entirely evaporated. Cover tightly; set aside, and let steam until every grain is separated. When ready to serve, use a fork in removing the rice from the cooking utensil.

[The foregoing recipe was given me by a lady of South Carolina, of great experience in the preparation of this staple cereal product of the Southern Atlantic seaboard.]

Stewed Okra.

Cut into pieces one quart of okra, and put to boil in one cup of water; add a little onion and some tomatoes; salt and pepper to taste; and when all is boiled tender, add a good lump of butter, worked in with a spoonful of flour, and let stew five minutes, stirring frequently.

Bread, Cakes, Pies, Puddings and Pastry.
SOLID AND LIQUID SAUCES.

Quick Bread.

Mix 2 teaspoonfuls baking powder with quart of flour, adding 1 teaspoonful salt and sufficient milk or water to make a soft dough, and bake at once in a hot oven. If eaten hot, break; use a hot knife in cutting.

Quick Muffins.

Take 2 eggs, 2 tablespoonfuls best lard or butter, 1 teaspoonful salt, 2 teaspoonfuls baking powder, 1 tablespoonful sugar, 1 quart good milk, and flour to make a moderately stiff batter, and bake at once in muffin-rings.

Brown Bread.

3 cups of yellow corn-meal, 1 cup flour, 2 sweet, and $\frac{1}{2}$ cup sour milk, with $\frac{1}{2}$ cup syrup, 1 teaspoonful soda, and a little salt. Bake 4 hours.

Graham Rolls.

Two cups graham and 1 of white flour, $\frac{1}{2}$ cup of yeast or $\frac{1}{3}$ cake compressed yeast, 2 teaspoonfuls sugar; mix with warm milk or water, and let stand upon range until light.

Mississippi River Corn-Bread.

One pint best yellow corn-meal, 1 pint of butter-milk, 2 tablespoonfuls melted butter, 2 eggs and teaspoonful of salt, 1 teaspoonful saleratus; mix well, and bake at a brisk fire.

Nice Light Biscuit.

Before sifting 1 quart of flour, put in 2 or 3 teaspoonfuls of best baking powder, adding a little salt after sifting. Follow this with 3 tablespoonfuls of best lard, and with good milk, mix into soft dough—working as little as possible. Roll full half-an-inch thick; cut and bake in a hot oven until slightly browned on top and bottom.

Clayton's Corn-Bread.

Take 3 cups of good corn-meal—either yellow or white—and 1 cup of flour; add a teaspoonful of baking powder, stirring well together. Next, put into a vessel, 2 eggs, well beaten, 1 tablespoonful of sugar, a little salt, a large tablespoonful of sweet lard or butter, and milk enough to make a thick batter. Let these come to a boiling heat, stirring well at the same time, then pour in the meal, and beat to a stiff consistence. Turn into a baking pan, and bake until thoroughly done, brown on top and bottom. Use hot milk in mixing, as, in my opinion, it takes the raw taste from the corn-meal.

Johnny Cake.

Two spoonfuls of melted butter, 1 egg, well beaten, 2 teaspoonfuls baking powder, 2 cups milk, $\frac{1}{2}$ cup sugar or syrup, 2 cups each, corn-meal and flour. Bake in a moderate oven until brown.

Sweet Potato Pone.

One large sweet potato grated, 1 cup yellow Indian meal, 2 eggs, 1 tablespoonful butter, $\frac{1}{2}$ cup molasses, $\frac{1}{2}$ cup sugar, salt and spice to taste; add sufficient milk to make the usual thickness of cake.

Ginger-Bread.

One pint molasses, $\frac{1}{2}$ pint of sour milk, 2 teaspoonfuls ginger, 1 teacup butter, 1 teaspoonful soda, 2 eggs—salt.

Molasses Ginger Bread.

One cup syrup, ½ cup sugar, ½ cup sweet milk, 2 tablespoonfuls vinegar, ½ cup shortening; flour to make moderately thick, and large teaspoonful baking powder.

Quaker Cake.

One cup butter, 3 teaspoonfuls ginger, 5 flour, ½ cup cider or any spirits, 4 eggs, and a teaspoonful of saleratus, dissolved in a teacup of sweet milk.

Pound Cake.

One cup sugar, ½ cup best butter, ½ cup of rich milk or cream, 3 eggs, well beaten, 1½ cups flour, 1 large teaspoonful baking powder, and a teaspoonful ground nutmeg; and beat the whole thoroughly before baking.

Chocolate Cake.—Jelly Cake.

Two cups sugar, 1 cup butter, the yolks of 5 eggs, and whites of 2, 1 cup pure milk, 3½ cups flour, 1 teaspoonful cream of tartar, ½ teaspoonful bi-carbonate soda, and stir thoroughly before baking.

The following is the mixture for filling.

Whites of 3 eggs, 1½ cups sugar, 3 tablespoonfuls of grated chocolate, and 1 teaspoonful extract vanilla. Beat well together, and spread between each layer and on top the cake.

[Jelly cake may be made the same way, using jelly instead of chocolate.]

Currant Cake.

Three eggs, 2 cups sugar, 1 butter, 1 milk, ½ teaspoonful soda, 1 cup currants, and a little citron, cut in thin slices, with flour to make a stiff batter. Pour into pans, and bake medium quick.

CREAM CUP-CAKE.

Four cups of flour, 2 of sugar, 3 of sweet cream, 4 eggs; mix and bake in square tins. When cold, cut in squares about two inches wide.

JUMBLES.

Rub to a cream a pound of butter and a pound of sugar; mix with a pound and a half of flour, 4 eggs and a little brandy; roll the cakes in powdered sugar, lay in flat buttered tins, and bake in a quick oven.

SWEET CAKE.

One cup of sugar, 1 cup sour cream, 1 cup butter, 1 egg, $\frac{1}{2}$ teaspoonful soda, $\frac{1}{2}$ nutmeg grated fine, flour enough to make a stiff batter. Bake in a slow oven.

SPONGE CAKE.

Five eggs, 2 cups sugar, 2 cups flour, $\frac{1}{2}$ teacup cold water; mix well and bake quickly.

GINGER SNAPS.

Into 1 pint of molasses put 1 cup lard, 1 tablespoonful of ginger, 1 teaspoonful of soda, and a little salt; boil for a few minutes, and when quite cool, add sufficient flour to make a stiff dough; roll very thin and bake.

A NICE CAKE.

One quart flour, 4 eggs, $\frac{1}{2}$ cup butter, $\frac{1}{2}$ cup sweet lard, 2 teaspoonfuls of baking powder, and 1 of salt. Beat the whites and yolks of the eggs separately, until light. Sift the baking powder into the flour. Melt the shortening in a cup of milk with the yolks of the eggs—putting the whites in last. Work into a thick batter, and bake steadily for three-quarters of an hour; to be eaten hot.

ICING FOR CAKE.

There are a number of formulas for the preparation of icings for cake, but the following will invariably be found the simplest, easiest prepared, and the best:

Take the whites of 4 eggs, and 1 pound of best pulverized white sugar, and any flavoring extract most agreeable to the taste. Break the whites of the eggs into a broad, cool dish, and after throwing a small handful of sugar upon them, begin whipping it in with long even strokes of the beater. Beat until the icing is of a smooth, fine and firm texture. If not stiff enough, put in more sugar, using at least a quarter of a pound to each egg. Pour the icing by the spoonful on top of the cake, and near the centre of the surface to be covered. If the loaf is so shaped that the liquid will naturally settle to its place, it is best left to do so. To spread it, use a broad-bladed knife, dipped in cold water; if as thick with sugar as should be, one coat will be amply sufficient. Leave in a moderate oven for three minutes. To color icing yellow, use the rind of a lemon or orange, tied in a thin muslin bag, straining a little of the juice through it and squeezing hard into the ice and sugar; for red, use extract of cochineal.

CHOCOLATE ICING.

Quarter of a cake of chocolate grated, $\frac{1}{2}$ cup of sweet milk, 1 tablespoonful corn-starch; flavor with extract of vanilla. Mix these ingredients, with the exception of the vanilla; boil two minutes, and after it has fairly commenced to boil, flavor, and then sweeten to taste with powdered sugar, taking care to have it sweet enough.

LEMON PIE.

Grated rind and juice of two lemons; 2 cups sugar; butter, the size of an egg; 2 tablespoonfuls corn-starch; 4 eggs. Rub the butter and sugar smooth in a little cold water; have ready 2 cups boiling water, in which stir the corn-starch, until it looks clear; add to this the butter and sugar, and, when nearly cold, the yolks of four eggs, and the white of one, well beaten, and the rind and the juice of the lemons. After lining two deep dishes with a delicate paste, and pouring in the mixture, beat the remaining whites of the eggs to a stiff froth, adding two spoonfuls of powdered sugar. Spread this over the pies when done, returning to the oven to brown.

English Plum Pudding.

Three cups flour; 2 eggs; 1 cup milk; ½ cup brandy; 1 nutmeg; a teaspoonful of salt; 5 teaspoonfuls baking powder; ½ pound currants; ½ pound raisins, stoned and chopped fine; ½ pound suet chopped fine; 1 cup sugar. Boil three hours.

Baked Apple Pudding.

Two cups oatmeal or cracked wheat; 2 eggs; 1 tablespoonful butter; 1 pint milk; three medium-sized apples; a little suet; cinnamon to flavor; sweeten to taste. Beat sugar, eggs, and milk together; stir in the meal, and then add the other ingredients, the apples last, after reducing to small pieces. Bake until well set. To be eaten with or without sauce.

Bread Pudding.

One loaf of stale bread, soaked in a pint of milk, and when soft, beat with an egg-beater until very fine. Pour into this the yolks of four eggs, well beaten, a tablespoonful of butter, some flavoring, and a little salt, beating all well together. After baking until well set, let it cool, and spread a nice jelly over the top, and on this put the whites of the eggs, beaten to a stiff froth, returning to the oven to brown.

Baked Corn-Meal Pudding.

Into a large cup of corn-meal stir 1 pint scalded milk; a small cup suet, chopped fine; two-thirds of a cup of syrup or molasses; salt to taste, and when cold, add 1 pint milk, and 2 eggs, well beaten, 1 teaspoonful cinnamon, and 1 cup raisins. Bake three hours.

Corn-Starch Pudding (Baked).

Four tablespoonfuls corn-starch; 1 quart of milk; 2 eggs; $\frac{3}{4}$ coffee-cup white sugar; adding butter size of an egg, with flavoring to taste. After dissolving the corn-starch in a little cold water, heat the milk to boiling and stir this in, and boil three minutes, stirring the mixture all the time; next, stir in the butter, and set away until cold. Beat the eggs until very light, when add the sugar and seasoning, and then stir into the corn-starch, beating thoroughly to a smooth custard. Put into a buttered dish, and bake not more than half an hour. This pudding is best eaten cold, with sauce made of cream and sugar, flavored with nutmeg or cinnamon, or both, or plain powdered sugar, as tastes may prefer.

DELMONICO PUDDING.

One quart of milk; 3 tablespoonfuls corn-starch; put in hot water until it thickens; to the yolks of 5 eggs, add three tablespoonfuls white sugar, 2 tablespoonfuls vanilla, and a little salt. Pour on the corn-starch, stir thoroughly, and bake fifteen minutes, but not long enough to whey. Beat the whites of the eggs to a stiff froth; add 3 tablespoonfuls of sugar; $\frac{1}{2}$ teaspoonful vanilla; put on top, and let brown.

PEACH ICE-CREAM.

Pare and cut in pieces 1 dozen peaches, or more, if desired, and boil with $\frac{1}{2}$ pound loaf sugar. When reduced to a marmalade press through a fine sieve, and when cool, add 1 pint cream and freeze. Serve with halves or quarters of fresh peaches, half frozen, around the cream.

APPLE SNOW.

Reduce half a dozen apples to a pulp; press them through a sieve; add $\frac{1}{2}$ cup powdered sugar and a teaspoonful lemon extract; take whites of 6 eggs and whip several minutes, and sprinkle 2 tablespoonfuls powdered sugar over them; beat the apple-pulp to a froth and add the beaten eggs. Whip the mixture well until it breaks like stiff snow, then pile it high in rough portions, in a glass dish—garnish with a spoonful of currant jelly.

Strawberry Sauce.

A delicious sauce for baked pudding: Beat ½ cup butter and 1 of sugar, to a cream; add, stiff beaten, white of 1 egg and a large cupful of ripe strawberries, thoroughly crushed.

Ambrosia.

Have ready a grated cocoanut and some oranges, peeled and sliced; put a large layer of oranges in your dish, and strew sugar over them; then a layer of cocoanut, then orange, and sprinkle sugar; and so on until the dish is full, having cocoanut for the last layer. Pine-apple may be substituted for the orange.

Farina Pudding.

Two tablespoonfuls farina, soaked in a little milk for two hours; 1 quart of milk. Set in a kettle of boiling water; when the milk boils, add the farina, stirring four minutes. Then stir in the yolks of 5 eggs, well beaten, 1 cup sugar, and a little salt. After boiling three or four minutes, pour into a dish to cool. Flavor, and stir in the whites of the eggs beaten to a foam. To be eaten cold.

Baked Corn-Meal Pudding.

Take 1 large teacupful of corn-meal; scald 1 pint of milk, and stir the meal in slowly and thoroughly. Add a small cup of suet, chopped fine; ⅔ of a cup of molasses, salt to taste, and when cool add 1 pint milk, with 2 eggs, well beaten, 1 teaspoonful of cinnamon and 1 cup of raisins. Bake 3 hours.

Snow Pudding.

One box gelatine, 2 cups sugar, juice of 2 lemons, whites of 3 eggs, 1 quart of milk, 5 eggs, 5 tablespoonfuls sugar, and 1 vanilla. Dissolve the gelatine in ¼ pint of water and let stand for 2 hours; then add ¼ pint of boiling water, the lemon juice, and sugar; strain and set away to cool and thicken, and when quite stiff, add the whites of the 3 eggs, beaten to a stiff froth; stir these into the jelly until it looks like snow—mould and set on ice.

For a similar custard; add 5 eggs, well beaten in a dish, with 5 tablespoonfuls white sugar.

Fruit Pudding.

One quart of flour, 2 teaspoonfuls yeast powder, a little salt, 1 cup suet chopped fine, or a $\frac{1}{4}$ pound butter or sweet lard; mix to soft dough, and roll quite thin—spreading over any kind of cooked fruit, sweetened to taste—rolling up nicely. This may be boiled, but is much better steamed, as this makes it much lighter. This delicious pudding should be eaten with brandy or wine sauce, liquid or solid.

Charlotte-a-Russe.

Take 1 pint rich milk, $\frac{1}{2}$ ounce of gelatine, dissolved in a little hot milk, the whites of 2 eggs beaten to a froth, and 1 cup sugar; flavoring with vanilla. Mix the milk, eggs, sugar and flavoring; and when the gelatine is cold, pour it in, stirring thoroughly. Line the dish or mould with slices of sponge cake, fill with this mixture, and set on ice to cool.

Solid Sauce.

Work well into $\frac{1}{2}$ cup of the freshest butter, 1 cup of powdered white sugar, adding the white of an egg, well beaten, and worked in with a large spoonful of California brandy, or a couple of spoonfuls of good sherry or California white-wine; working all of these well together, that the ingredients may be thoroughly incorporated, and season with nutmeg or cinnamon, or both, as may be preferred.

Liquid Sauce.

Take butter, the size of an egg, and sufficient flour or corn-starch, and after adding boiling water to make thick drawn butter, boil two or three minutes;

add brandy, sherry or white-wine—according to taste—with a little vinegar or juice of 1 lemon. Make quite sweet and season to taste.

Currant, or Grape Jelly.

Wash the currants or grapes well in a pan of water; afterwards mash thoroughly, and put in a preserving kettle, letting them simmer slowly for fifteen or twenty minutes. Strain through a thin muslin bag, and, for every pint of juice, add one pound of granulated sugar. Mix well together, and boil five minutes, and put into glasses while warm. Cut paper to fit the top, dip in brandy, and lay over the jelly, and when quite cold tie a paper over the top, and put away in a dry, dark place.

Calves' Foot Jelly.

Boil 4 calves' feet in 4 or 5 quarts of water, until reduced to shreds; strain, and let the liquid cool; after taking off the fat, put the jelly in a kettle, with one pint of California sherry, or white wine, 3 cups granulated sugar, the whites of 4 eggs, well beaten, the juice of 1 lemon, with half of the grated peel, 1 teaspoonful of ground cinnamon or nutmeg; boil until clear, and strain into moulds or glasses.

Ice-Cream.

There are a thousand and one modes and recipes for making ice-cream. But, after having tested the merits of a large number, I have found the following formula, used by Mr. Piper, the former head cook of the Occidental Hotel, of San Francisco, in all respects superior to any that I have ever used:

One quart of Jersey, or best dairy milk, with the addition of a pint of rich cream; 6 eggs, and 1 pound of best granulated white sugar, thoroughly beaten and incorporated together; place the milk in a can, set it in a vessel of boiling water, and let it come to a boiling heat, stirring well at the same time. Then take from the fire, and add vanilla, lemon, or such flavoring as you may prefer, after which set it in ice-water to cool, and then freeze. Break the ice for the freezer of a uniform size, mixing coarse salt with the mass. Stir the cream constantly, and scrape thoroughly from the sides. The more the cream is stirred, the more delicate the mixture will be.

ORANGE-ICE.

The juice of 6 oranges; after adding the grated rind of 1 mix the juice of two lemons, and the grated rind of one; after adding 1 pint of granulated white sugar, dissolved in a pint of cold water, freeze the mixture the same as ice cream.

LEMON JELLY.

One pound sugar; 3 lemons, sliced, and put into the sugar; 1 ounce gelatine, dissolved in cold water sufficient to cover; add a quart of boiling water, and strain into moulds.

WINE JELLY.

One box Cox's gelatine, dissolved in a little warm water; add a large goblet sherry wine, and $1\frac{1}{2}$ pints of boiling water; sweeten highly and boil briskly. To be eaten with cream.

PEACH JELLY.

Do not pare, but rub your peaches; place them in a porcelain lined kettle, with just enough water to cover. Let them cook thoroughly—from one to two hours—then strain through a jelly-bag. To every 4 cups of juice, add 3 cups of sugar, and set on to boil again. Sometimes, when the fruit is particularly fine and fresh, three-quarters of an hour or less boiling is sufficient to make a jelly, but sometimes it takes longer. To test it, drop some in a saucer and set on ice; if it does not spread but remain rounded, it is done.

ROMAN PUNCH.

Take the juice of 4 oranges, and of the same number of lemons or limes. Dissolve 1 pound of white sugar in a pint of water. Mix all these together, and strain; after which add 1 pint of California champagne, and 2 gills of good California brandy, if desirable. Freeze the same as ice-cream.

MISCELLANEOUS.

BUTTER AND BUTTER-MAKING.

With the exception of bread, which has been appropriately termed "the staff of life," there is, perhaps, no other article of food more universally used by mankind than butter. Notwithstanding this well established fact, it is a lamentable reflection, that really good butter is one of the rarest and most difficult articles to be procured. Although the adulterations of this staple article of food are numerous, the main cause of the quantities of bad butter with which the community is burdened, is ignorance of the true methods, and slovenliness in the preparation of this staple article, for which no reasonable excuse can be urged. In the making of good butter, no process is more simple or easily accomplished. The Quakers, living in the vicinity of Philadelphia, more than a century ago, so thoroughly understood and practised the art of making the best butter, that the products of their dairies sold readily in that city for from five to eight cents per pound more than that produced by any other class.

With these thrifty people, cleanliness was really regarded as "akin to godliness," and the principal was thoroughly and practically carried out in all their every day affairs. The most scrupulous attention being paid to the keeping of all the utensils used scrupulously clean, and so thoroughly work the mass, that every particle of milk is expelled. The greatest evil to be guarded against, is the too free use of salt, which for this purpose should be of the utmost purity and refined quality. I am satisfied, from personal observation, that the butter made at the Jersey Farm, at San Bruno, in the vicinity of San Francisco, in every respect equals in quality the celebrated Darlington, Philadelphia.

For the keeping milk fresh and sweet, and the proper setting of the rich cream, an old style spring-house is essentially requisite. Who that has ever visited one of these clean, cool and inviting appendages of a well conducted farm and well ordered household, at some home-farm of the olden time, does not recall it in the mind's-eye, as vividly as did the poet Woodworth when he penned that undying poem of ancient home-life, "The Old Oaken Bucket that Hung in the Well."

Properly constructed, a spring-house should be built of stone, which is regarded as the coolest—brick or concrete—with walls at least twelve inches in thickness. The floor should be of brick, and not more than two feet below the surface of the ground. The roof should be of some material best adapted to warding off the heat, and keeping the interior perfectly cool, while due attention should be paid to the allowance of a free circulation of air, and provision be made for thorough ventilation; only as much light as is actually necessary should be admitted, and where glass is used for this purpose, it should invariably be shielded from the sun. Walled trenches being constructed for this purpose, a constant stream of cool running water should pass around the pans containing the milk and cream, which, for the making of good butter, should never be permitted to become sour. The shelving and other furniture, and all wooden utensils used, should be of white ash, maple or white wood, in order to avoid all danger of communicating distasteful or deleterious flavors. As there is no liquid more sensitive to its surroundings, or which more readily absorbs the flavor of articles coming in contact with it, than pure milk, everything that has a tendency to produce this deleterious result should be carefully excluded. Neither paints or varnish should be used about the structure, and the entire concern should be as utterly free from paint as the inside of an old time Quaker meeting-house.

In making butter, the cream should be churned at a temperature of about 65 degrees. When the churning is finished, take up the lump and carefully work out every particle of milk. Never wash or put your hands in the mass. To each pound of butter work in a little less than an ounce of the purest dairy salt. Set the butter away, and at the proper time work the mass over until not a particle of milk remains.

A Word of Advice to Hotel and Restaurant Cooks.

I wish to say a word to the extensive brotherhood and ancient and honorable guild constituting the Grand Army of Hotel and Restaurant Cooks distributed throughout our country, on the all-important subject of making coffee and heating milk. Some satirical writer has sarcastically said that the way to make good coffee is to ascertain how that beverage is prepared in leading hotels and restaurants, and then make your coffee as they don't! There is no good reason why coffee cannot be as well made in hotel and restaurant kitchens, as in private families or anywhere else, if the berry is good, well-browned, and pains are taken for the proper preparation of this popular beverage.

Twenty years ago the art of making coffee in large quantities, and of properly heating milk for the same, was an unsolved problem—in fact, if not numbered among the many lost arts, might be classed as among the unknown in the culinary art. Twenty-one years ago, the late Mr. Marden—a well-known citizen of San Francisco—and the author of this work—produced, as the result of long practical experience, a form for making a decoction of the ancient Arabian berry, which is now in general use throughout the entire Union. True, attempts have been made to improve upon the mode, which was the crowning triumph of the parties alluded to, but they have invariably proved failures, and to-day Marden & Clayton's coffee and milk urns stand pre-eminent in this important department of cookery. These urns are simply two capacious stone-ware jars, of equal capacity, and made precisely alike, with an orifice one inch from the bottom, in which a faucet is firmly cemented. Each jar is suspended in a heavy tin casing, affording an intervening space of two inches, which is to be filled with hot, but not boiling water, as a too high temperature would injure the flavor of the coffee, and detract from the aroma of the fragrant berry. Suspend a thin cotton sack in the centre, and half the height of the jar. After putting in this the desired amount of coffee, pour on it sufficient boiling water to make strong coffee. As soon as the water has entirely filtered through, draw off the liquid through the stop-cock at the bottom of the jar, and return it to the sack, passing it through, in the same manner, two or three times. After five minutes raise the sack, pour in a cup of hot water, and let it filter through, getting, in this manner, every particle of the strength. Immediately after this remove the sack; for if it is left remaining but a short time, the aroma will be changed for the worse. Cover tightly, and keep the jar surrounded with hot, but not boiling water. Next, put into the milk urn—also surrounded with hot water—one-half the milk for the amount of coffee, and at the proper time add the remaining half of the milk, having it, in this manner, fresh, and not over-cooked. Should the milk become too hot, pour in a cup of cold milk, stirring well at the same time.

The first of these urns for making coffee and heating milk, were those used for the purpose at the opening of the Occidental Hotel of this city—of which Mr. Piper was at that time the intelligent and experienced head-cook. This mode of making coffee in large quantities is still followed at this hotel, which, from the time of its opening to the present, has maintained the reputation as one of the best of the numerous excellent public houses of this city, and the entire Union.

Clayton's California Golden Coffee.

Let the coffee—which should be nicely browned, but not burned—be ground rather fine, in order that you may extract the strength without boiling—as that dissipates the aroma and destroys the flavor. Put the coffee in a thin muslin sack—reaching less than half-way to the bottom of the vessel—then place it in the pot, and pour over enough boiling water to make strong coffee. Let it stand on the hot range two or three minutes, when lift out the sack, pour the liquid in a vessel, and return it through the sack the second time, after which, raising the sack again, pour through a little hot water to extract all the strength from the grounds. Next, pour into the liquid, cold, Jersey Dairy, or any other pure country milk, until the coffee assumes a rich golden color, and after it reaches a boiling-heat once more, set it back. Should the milk be boiled separately, the richness, combined with its albumen, will be confined to the top; whereas, if added cold, and boiled with the coffee, it will be thoroughly incorporated with the liquid, adding materially to its rich flavor and delicate aroma.

[Never substitute a woolen for the muslin strainer, as that fabric, being animal should never come in contact with heat; while cotton or linen, being of vegetable fibre, is easily washed clean and dried. Neither should tin be used, as that lets the fine coffee through, and clouds the liquid, which should be clear. To extract its full strength, coffee should invariably be ground as fine as oatmeal or finely-ground hominy, and protracted boiling dissipates the aroma and destroys its fine flavor.]

The Very Best Way to Make Chocolate.

After grating through a coarse grater, put the chocolate in a stewpan with a coffee-cup or more of hot water; let it boil up two or three minutes, and add plenty of good rich country milk to make it of the right consistency. Too much water tends to make this otherwise delightful beverage insipid.

[Good Cocoa is made in the same manner.]

Old Virginia Egg-Nog.

Two dozen fresh eggs; 1 gallon rich milk; $1\frac{1}{2}$ pounds powdered sugar; 2 pints cognac brandy, or Santa Cruz rum—or $\frac{1}{2}$ pint cognac and $\frac{1}{2}$ pint Jamaica, or Santa Cruz rum. Break the eggs carefully, separating the whites from the yolks; add the sugar to the latter, and with a strong spoon beat until very light, adding gradually 2 dessert spoonfuls of powdered mace or nutmeg. Next, add the liquor, pouring in slowly, stirring actively at the same time; after which add the milk in like manner. Meanwhile—having whipped the whites of the eggs with an egg-beater into a light froth—pour the egg-nog into a bowl, add the white froth, and decorate with crimson sugar or nutmeg, and serve. The foregoing proportions will be sufficient to make fourteen pints of very superior egg-nog.

Clayton's Popular Sandwich Paste.

Take 2 pounds of Whittaker's Star ham, in small pieces—$\frac{2}{3}$ lean and $\frac{1}{3}$ fat—the hock portion of the ham is best for this purpose. Have ready two fresh calves tongues, boiled and skinned nicely, and cut like the ham. Put these in a kettle, along with 2 good-sized onions, and cover with cold water, boiling slowly until quite tender; when add 1 pound of either fresh or canned tomatoes, stirring for half-an-hour, adding a little hot water, if in danger of burning. Add to the mixture, at the same time, these spices: plenty of best mustard, and a little ground cloves, along with Worcestershire or Challenge sauce, allowing the mixture to simmer five minutes. When cool enough, pour into a wooden bowl, and after chopping fine, pound the mixture well, while it is warm, with a potato-masher. After the mass has cooled it will spread like butter. Should additional seasoning be desired, it can be worked in at any desired time. If not rich enough to suit some palates, one-fourth of a pound best butter may be worked in.

The bread used for the sandwiches must be quite cold and perfectly fresh—cutting carefully in thin slices—using for this purpose a long, thin-bladed and quite sharp knife. Take a thin shaving from the bottom of the loaf, then from the top an inch-wide slice, after removing the crust. Care must be taken to cut without either tearing or pressing the bread. Spread on one side of each slice—as if using butter—and after joining the slices, cut the same to suit the taste.

[As the best bread is the only kind to be used in making sandwiches—without wishing to make invidious distinctions—I must say that Engleberg furnishes from his bakery (on Kearney street), the best I have ever used for this purpose, as it cuts without breaking, and does not dry so soon as other breads I have made use of.]

Welsh Rabbit.

To prepare Welsh rabbit, or rare-bit—both names being used to designate this popular and appetizing dish, which has ever been a favorite with gourmands and good livers, both ancient and modern—take one-half pound of best cheese—not, however, over nine months old—Davidson's, Gilroy, California, or White's, Herkimer County, New York, and cut in small pieces. Put over a slow fire, in a porcelain-lined kettle; when it begins to melt pour in three tablespoonfuls rich milk or cream, and a little good mustard. Stir from the time the cheese begins to melt, to prevent scorching. Have ready a quite hot dish; cover the bottom with toast, buttered upon both sides, upon which pour the melted cheese, spreading evenly over. If you prefer, you may use as a condiment a little mustard, pepper or any favorite sauce. This is a dish that must be eaten as soon as taken from the fire.

Delicate Waffles.

Take ½ pound butter; ½ pound fine sugar; 9 eggs; 3 pints of milk; 1½ ounces of best baking powder, and 2¼ pounds sifted flour. Beat the butter and sugar to a cream; add the yolks of the eggs, the milk, and half the flour; mix well, with the whites of the eggs, beaten to a staunch snow, and add the remainder of the flour. Bake in waffle irons, well greased and heated. When baked, the tops may be dusted well with fine sugar, or with a mixture of sugar and powdered cinnamon.

Force-Meat Balls.

Mix, with 1 pound of chopped veal, or other meat, 1 egg, a little butter, 1 cup, or less, of bread crumbs—moistening the whole with milk or the juice of the stewed meat. Season with summer savory. Make into small balls, and fry brown.

Beef-Tea.

Take 3 pounds of lean beef; chop as fine as coarse hominy, and put in a vessel, covering the meat with cold water. Cover the vessel tightly, and let boil for four hours, carefully keeping the beef just covered with the water. Pass through a colander, pressing out all the juice with a potato-masher, strain through a cotton cloth, and add a little salt. A glass of sherry wine decidedly improves beef-tea.

Crab Sandwich.

Put ½ pound boiled crab meat in a mortar, and pound to a smooth paste, adding the juice of a lemon. Season with pepper and salt, with a pinch of curry powder, and mix the paste well with 6 ounces best butter. Cut slices of bread rather thin, trim off the crust, and spread.

Something about Pork.—The Kind to Select, and Best Mode of Curing.

The best quality of pork, as a matter of course, is that fed and slaughtered in the country. Corn, or any kind of grain-fed, or, more especially, milk-fed pork, as every one knows, who is not of the Hebrew faith, which entirely ignores this—when properly prepared, well-flavored, oleaginous production

—and is fond of pork, from the succulent sucking pig, the toothsome and fresh spare-rib, unrivalled as a broil, to the broiled or boiled ham, and side-meat bacon of the full-grown porker, is vastly superior to the meat of the slop and garbage-fed animal raised and slaughtered in the city—more especially as the butchering of hogs in San Francisco is at this time entirely monopolized by the Chinese population, who seem to have a warm side, in fact a most devoted affection, for the hog, surpassing even that of the bog-trotters of the "Ould Sod" for the traditional pet-pig that "ates, drinks and slapes wid the ould man, the ould woman, and the childer." Charles Lamb's account of the discovery of the delights of roast pig, and invention of that luxury by the Chinaman whose bamboo hut was burned down, in raking his pig, semi-cremated from the ashes, burned his fingers—which, naturally clapping into his mouth to ease the pain—which was changed to delight, causing John's torture-smitten visage to assume in an instant a broad grin of satisfaction at the discovery—is undoubtedly correct, or at least the love for the pork exhibited by the "Heathen Chinee" cannot reasonably be accounted for in any other way. In order, then, to get the best article of pork—wholesome, toothsome, and, what is most important of all, entirely free from any form of disease or taint, great care should be taken to make selections from the small lots fed and slaughtered in the country, and brought into the city most generally in the fall season, and which are to be procured at the stall or shop of any reputable and reliable dealer. Select a carcass of one hundred, or less, pounds, with flesh hard and white, and thin skin. For salting, cut in pieces six by eight inches, and, after having rubbed thoroughly in salt—neither too fine nor too coarse—take a half-barrel, sprinkle the bottom well with salt, and lay the pieces of pork in tightly; then add salt, and follow with another layer of pork, until the whole is packed, with salt sprinkled on top. Set in a cool place, and, after three or four days, make a brine of boiling water with salt—which, when cool, should be sufficiently strong to float an egg—stir in a half pound of brown sugar, pour over the meat sufficient to cover, and place on top a stone heavy enough to keep the pork weighted down.

Home-Made Lard.

Home-made lard is undoubtedly the best as well as cheapest. If leaf is not to be had, take 10 lbs of solid white pork, as fat as possible, which is quite as good, if not better; cut in pieces uniformly the size of your finger, and put in a vessel with a thick bottom—one of iron is preferable—and adding 1 pint of water, put on the range; keep tightly covered until the water has evaporated in steam, when leave off the cover, letting it cook slowly, until the scraps turn a light brown, when take off, and while still quite warm, strain through a colander, pressing the scraps hard with a potato-masher; pour the liquid into cans and set away. The next day it will be found snow-white, solid and of a fine and equal consistence; and for cooking purposes, quite as good as fresh churned butter in making biscuits, any kind of pastry, or frying eggs.

[In frying lard keep a careful watch and see that it does not scorch.]

New Jersey Sausage.

Take the very best pork you can get—one-third fat and two-thirds lean—and chop on a block with a kitchen cleaver. When half chopped, season with black pepper, salt and sage, rubbed through a sieve, and then finish the chopping; but do not cut the meat too fine, as in that case the juice of the meat will be lost. Make the mixture up into patties, and fry on a common pan, placed in the oven of the stove, taking care not to cook them hard. Veal is a good substitute for the lean pork in making these sausages, which are much better if made one day before cooking.

Pot-Pie.

The following I have found the best manner of making any kind of pot-pie. White meat, such as chicken, quail or nice veal, is decidedly the best for the purpose. Stew the meat until tender, in considerable liquid as when you put into the paste much of that will be absorbed. In making the paste take 1 quart of flour and 2 tablespoonfuls of baking powder, rubbed well into the flour, $\frac{1}{4}$ pound butter or sweet lard, and a little salt; mix with milk or water into a soft dough; roll $\frac{1}{2}$ an inch thick; cut to size, and lay in a steamer for 15 minutes to make light, then put in and around the stew; cooking slowly for ten minutes.

Curried Crab.

Put into a saucepan $\frac{1}{4}$ pound butter with a little flour; cook together and stir till cool; then add a gill of cream, a little cayenne pepper, salt, and a dessert-spoonful of East India Curry Powder. Mix well together, and add 1 pound boiled crab meat, chopped fine; stir well together—make very hot and serve. The addition of a glass of white wine adds to the flavor of this curry.

To Toast Bread.

Cut bread in slices $\frac{1}{2}$ an inch thick; first taking a thin crust from top, bottom and sides, or shave the loaf before cutting—otherwise the crust will scorch before the soft part is sufficiently toasted.

Cream Toast.

To make a delicious cream toast, mix well a teaspoonful of corn-starch with a little cold milk, and put in a stewpan with a piece of butter the size of an egg. Pour in hot milk, and stir two minutes, adding a little salt—a little sugar is also an improvement—and pour over the toast while hot.

Fritters.

Four eggs, well beaten; 1 quart of milk; 1 quart of flour; 2 teaspoonfuls baking powder; one tablespoonful sugar, and a little salt. Cook in best lard, and serve with hard or liquid sauce, highly flavored with California brandy or white wine.

Hash.

It is a mistaken idea (labored under by many), that hash can be made of waste material, that would otherwise be thrown away. This is a most excellent and palatable dish if properly prepared. Take the shank, or other parts of good beef you may have at hand, and boil, with as little water as possible, until quite tender, and let stand until quite cold. Then take of potatoes, that have been peeled before boiling, one-third the amount of the meat used, and chop moderately fine, adding plenty of pepper and salt, to taste. Next, chop two or three onions fine, and stew them in some of the liquid in which the meat was boiled, dredging in a little flour, and when thoroughly done, put in the hash, and chop and mix thoroughly. If you think the mass requires moistening add a little of the fat and juice. Put the whole in a pan, and bake in a quick oven until slightly browned at top and bottom.

Should you have good corned-beef—not too salt—it is very nice made in this manner. Use the marrow from the bones in making hash.

Hashed Potatoes with Eggs.

Chop fine 8 or 10 cold boiled potatoes; heat a pan (cast-iron is preferable,) quite hot; put in butter the size of an egg, and as soon as melted add the potatoes; salt and pepper; slightly stirring frequently, and, when heated thoroughly, stir in four well-beaten eggs. Serve on a hot dish.

Baked Macaroni.

Break the macaroni rather short; wash and put in salted water; boil about twenty minutes. Drain off the water, replace it with a cup of good milk and 1 tablespoonful of best butter, and as soon as boiling hot put in a baking-dish. If you like cheese, grate over it the best California article—old cheese should never be used—and bake to a light brown.

For stewed macaroni omit the baking and the cheese, if you like.

Drawn-Butter.

To make drawn-butter, take two tablespoonfuls of flour; good butter, the size of an egg; a little milk, and make to a smooth paste. Then work in slowly one-half pint of water, until the flour is cooked. Season to taste. The foregoing will be found a good basis for nearly all hot sauces, for fish, beet, and other vegetables, as well as for puddings.

Spiced Currants.

Two boxes of currants, washed and stemmed; 3 pounds sugar, 1 tablespoonful allspice, 1 tablespoonful of cloves, 1 tablespoonful cinnamon; boil half-an-hour.

THE BEST METHOD OF CANNING FRUITS.

There are various modes of canning fruits, almost every housekeeper having a method of her own. For the benefit of those who are at loss in this particular, we give the following mode—which we fully endorse as the best within our knowledge—made use of by Mrs. George W. Ladd, of Bradford, Massachusetts, whose fruits, prepared in this way, have repeatedly taken the first premium at the Agricultural Fair, held in the Old Bay State. This lady certainly deserves the thanks of all interested in this important matter, for her liberality in giving the public the benefit of her knowledge and experience in this line, as detailed in the following, published in the *New York Graphic* of August 15, 1883:

"As the season of ripe fruit advances, I prepare such quantities of syrup as I think I may need, in this way: Three pounds of granulated sugar to one gallon of water and boil twenty minutes; this I put in glass jars, when cool, and set away for future use. Peaches, quinces, pears, apples, plums, pine apples, rhubarb, crab apples, and, in fact, all fruits of this kind, I peel, quarter and place in a dish of cold water (to prevent discoloration), until I have prepared enough to fill a jar: I then pack them solid as possible in a jar, and then fill the jar with the syrup previously prepared. I then place a wire stand in the bottom of my preserving kettle, on which to place the jar, then fill the kettle with cold water until the jar is two-thirds covered; leave the jar open, but cover the kettle and boil until the fruit is sufficiently soft; have ready a little boiling syrup, if needed, to fill the jar full to overflowing. Then place the rubber band around the neck of the jar and screw the cover on as tightly as possible; then in from three to five minutes give the cover another turn, in order to be sure it is air tight, and you will have no mortal trouble with it. I use Mason's jars with metallic porcelain covers."

PREPARING QUINCES FOR CANNING OR PRESERVING.

Quinces for canning or preserving should be kept in a dry place for thirty days after taking from the trees, in order to give them richness and flavor. Peel and cut to the proper size, carefully saving skins and cores. Put the last named in a porcelain kettle and boil until quite tender, when strain through a cotton-bag; afterwards put the juice back in the kettle, and add sugar as directed in the directions for canning fruit. Boil slowly for half-an-hour, taking off the scum as it rises, then set away to cool, and can the fruit as directed in the receipt for canning.

Clayton's Monmouth Sauce.

In making this delightful ketchup, take 25 pounds of fresh, or two 8 lb. cans of tomatoes, and slice, not too thin, adding five medium sized onions cut fine. Put these, with plenty of salt, in a porcelain kettle; adding, with a handful of hot green peppers, or a less quantity, if dried, 1 ounce of white ginger, chopped fine, 1 ounce of horse-radish, and $\frac{1}{2}$ ounce each of ground cloves and allspice, and 1 lemon, with seeds removed and cut small. After letting these boil for three hours, work through a sieve and return to the kettle along with a pint of wine vinegar, 2 tablespoonfuls sugar, 2 of good mustard, a teacupful of Challenge or Worcestershire Sauce, and let boil for 2 or 3 minutes, and set off. To prevent fermentation, stir in a teacupful of high-proof California brandy. If too thick, when cold reduce with vinegar.

To Prepare Mustard for the Table.

Take $\frac{1}{2}$ pound best mustard and enough wine vinegar, mixed with $\frac{1}{3}$ boiling water, 1 large teaspoonful of salt, 1 teaspoonful of sugar, juice of half a lemon, and mix to a thin batter, and put in a common glass jar and keep stopped tight. If pure mustard is used, treated in this way, it will keep good for months.

[If you desire the best article of mustard, I think E. R. Durkee & Co's is the best I have ever used, although Colman's ranks equally high, if you can get the genuine unadulterated article, which can be had by procuring Crosse & Blackwell's London brand, for which Messrs. Richards and Harrison are the San Francisco agents.]

Mint Sauce.

Into a teacupful of hot vinegar, in which has been dissolved sufficient sugar to make slightly sweet, add a handful of mint chopped quite fine. Serve hot.

Eggs Ought Never be Poached.

Poached eggs are always tasteless, and also unhealthy, owing to the albumen going into the water into which they are dropped, giving it a white and milky appearance—taking away a portion of the richness which should remain in the egg, rendering it indigestible, and of course, unwholesome.

Sunnyside Roast.

Select a good, tender piece either of beef or mutton—veal and pork can also be nicely roasted in the same way—place in your iron saucepan or pot one tablespoonful of good lard or half as much butter, and an onion, cut fine; let your onion fry to a light brown, and put in your meat, first having washed, dried and salted it. Put the cover on and let stand until it is pretty well browned; then add water, unless in danger of burning. Add only enough water, from time to time, to keep it from burning; turn it frequently so that it may brown on all sides. When tender, it will come forth brown and juicy. Just before serving, see that there is enough water for gravy; if there is not, you can take out the meat and add enough, but not too much, hot water, and then pour it over the meat.

Clayton's Spanish Omelette.

Chop into dice $\frac{1}{4}$ pound of breakfast bacon, a small tomato, 4 mushrooms, mince very fine a small onion; add pepper to taste, put in a frying pan and cook slowly until the lean is done; take off and put in a warm place to keep hot. This is sufficient for 6 eggs.

Plain Omelette.

Beat the yolks and white of 8 eggs separately until light, then beat together; add a little salt and 1 tablespoonful cream. Have in the pan a piece of butter, and when boiling hot pour in the omelette and shake until it begins to stiffen; then let it brown. Fold double and serve hot.

Clam Fritters.

Sift into an earthen dish 3 spoonfuls flour and ½ teaspoonful baking powder; add to this a little of the clam juice, ½ a cup of cream and 2 eggs, well beaten. Mince a pint of clams and mix with the batter. Put 2 or 3 spoonfuls of lard into a frying-pan, and when boiling, drop in the batter, by spoonfuls, to fry; after frying a minute, take from the pan, drain and serve.

Fried Tripe.

If the tripe is boiled tender, cut in pieces 2 inches square, season with salt and pepper and dip in a batter made of eggs, milk and flour, and fry in sweet lard, or drippings from roast or corned beef.

Ringed Potatoes.

Peel large potatoes, cut them round and round as you would pare an apple; fry in the best lard until a light brown; sprinkle with salt and serve hot.

New Potatoes Boiled.

Wash and rub new potatoes with a coarse towel, drop in boiling water, and boil until done, taking care that they are not over boiled. Have ready, in a saucepan, some milk or cream with butter, a little chopped parsley, pepper and salt; drain the potatoes, add them to the cream with a teaspoonful of corn-starch, soaked in a little milk; let it come to a simmer, and serve at once.

Fried Tomatoes.

Take large smooth tomatoes, cut them in slices $\frac{1}{2}$ an inch thick, dip in bread crumbs or cracker dust and fry a light brown, in half lard and half butter.

Squash and Corn.—Spanish Style.

Take 3 small summer squashes and 3 ears of corn; chop the squashes and cut the corn from the cobs. Put into a saucepan a spoonful of lard or butter, and when very hot an onion; fry a little; add the corn and squash, 1 tomato and 1 green pepper, cut small, and salt to taste. Cover closely and stir frequently to prevent scorching.

Pickles.

To make mixed pickles, cut small cucumbers crosswise in about 4 pieces; onions, if not very small, in 2, and peppers, if the ordinary size, in 4 pieces. Should you have green tomatoes, cut them small. Use a less amount of onions and peppers than cucumbers; mix all together with a few bay leaves. Next, take a tub or keg, and, having covered the bottom with fine salt, put on a layer of pickles, adding alternate layers of each, leaving that of salt on top. Cover with a cotton cloth, and lay on a stone or wooden weight. Let them remain three days; then take out, rinse in cold water, but do not soak, and put them in a basket or sack to drain for twelve hours. Have ready plenty of California wine vinegar, made hot, but not boiling, adding the following—cloves, allspice, green ginger, and whole mustard seed, with 1 coffee-cup sugar. When the vinegar is at scalding heat pour over the pickles and cover.

Nice Picklette.

Take 4 nice cabbages, chopped fine; 1 quart onions, chopped fine; 2 quarts —or sufficient to cover the mixture—best wine vinegar, adding two tablespoonfuls each of ground mustard, black pepper, cinnamon, celery salt, 1 of mace, and 1 coffee-cup sugar. Pack the cabbages and onions in alternate layers, with a little fine salt between, and let stand until next day; then scald the vinegar with the spices and sugar, and pour over the cabbages and onions. Repeat this the next day; and on the third, heat the whole scalding hot, let it cool, and put in jars, when it is fit for use at once.

Pickled Tripe.

Pickled tripe is very nice—and that sold by John Bayle, in the California Market, which is cleaned by steam process, and is quite tender and unsalted is a superior article. To prepare for pickling, cut in pieces about four inches square, say five or six pounds. Put into a kettle; cover with boiling water, adding a handful of salt; let stand fifteen minutes; take out and drain, keeping warm. Mix one-fourth water with the best wine vinegar—to which add cloves, allspice and mace, with 1 teacupful sugar; heat, and pour over the tripe, and set away to cool. Tripe prepared in this way is the best for broiling or frying.

To Cook Grouse or Prairie Chicken.

The best way I have found for cooking this delicious game bird is, first, after cleaning, to cut off the wings and legs, as, with the back, these parts are of little account; next, split the birds in the centre, taking out the breast-bone, and you have two heavy pieces; if the bird is large, divide again; do not wash, but wipe with a damp cloth. Season with pepper and salt, and broil with butter quite rare; then lay in a porcelain-lined pan, with butter and currant or grape jelly, adding a little cayenne pepper, and a small quantity of port or white wine.

[Venison steak may be cooked in the same manner.]

Brains and Sweet-Breads.

When properly prepared the brains of calves and sheep form a very inviting dish. Lay fresh brains in cold, salted water for fifteen minutes; then put them in boiling water, and parboil for ten minutes. After cleaning off the outer membrane—for frying—split them, and season with salt and pepper, and run them through egg, beaten with a little milk; roll them in cracker-dust, and fry to a light brown in equal parts of sweet lard and butter.

For stewed brains, cut half the size for frying and put in a stewpan, with a lump of butter, pepper and salt, a little water or soup-stock, and one-half an onion, chopped fine and stewed tender. Add this, and cook slowly for a few minutes, when put in two or three spoonfuls of milk or cream, and a little white wine or juice of lemon.

[Sweet-breads may be cooked in the same manner.]

Stewed Spare-Ribs of Pork.

Cut the ribs in pieces of a finger's length and the width of two fingers. Put in the kettle with two onions, salt and pepper, and cover with cold water. Let them stew slowly for two hours, and then put in 3 potatoes, 2 purple-top turnips, which have been peeled and cut, and left in cold water at least two hours; also add two tomatoes. This stew must have plenty of gravy, which can be made by working a little flour and butter with a few spoonfuls of rich milk, cooking five minutes.

[An Irish stew may be made in the foregoing manner by substituting ribs of mutton.]

Broiled Oysters.

In order to broil oysters properly, take those of the largest size, drain, and dry in a cloth, and lay carefully on a nice wire gridiron that will hold them tight; sprinkle slightly with salt and pepper, and put them over a good clear fire for a short time, and turn, taking care not to broil too much; serve with the best butter on a hot dish.

Pumpkin or Squash Custard.

Take enough pumpkin or squash to make 1 quart when cooked; and after it is boiled or steamed, rub through a sieve, and work in 3 eggs well beaten, with rich milk sufficient to make the proper consistence, adding sugar to taste; season with ginger and allspice, and bake in cups or dishes to a nice brown. May be eaten hot, but is better cold.

Fig Pudding.

Take 1 pint grated bread crumbs, 1 cup suet, 1 cup brown sugar, 2 eggs and ½ pound of fresh figs. Wash the figs in warm water, and dry in a cloth; chop the suet and figs together, and add the other ingredients, also 1 nutmeg, grated. Put in a mould or floured bag, and boil 3 hours. Serve with hard sauce.

Fried Apples.

Take 6 good cooking apples, cut in slices ¼ of an inch thick; have a pan of fresh hot lard ready, drop the slices in and fry brown; sprinkle a little sugar over them and serve hot.

Clayton's Oyster Stew.

In my long experience I have found that the best way to stew oysters, is, after having saved all the juice of the oysters, to put it in a stew pan with a little boiling water, and a good lump of butter worked in a little flour, adding pepper and salt. Let these boil for two minutes, or long enough to cook the flour; then put in the oysters, and the moment the stew boils up again add a little sweet cream or country milk, and when it boils the stew is cooked and should be set away from a hot fire. Cooked in this way, good oysters will never be tough and tasteless as is too often the case.

Boiled Celery.

Cut the white stalks of celery the length of asparagus, boil in as little salted water as possible until quite tender. The root, cut in slices, is equally good. Dress with drawn butter made with the water in which the celery was boiled. This vegetable is said to be a sedative and antidote to nervous debility.

Selecting Meats.

For a roast of beef, select from the ribs nearest the point of the shoulder-blade, running backward. For steaks, choose that with the diamond bone on either side. For chops of mutton or lamb, select the rib. For roasting, choose the loin or saddle; and for boiling, the leg of mutton—but not of lamb, the latter being best roasted. For corned-beef, select parts commonly known as the navel and plate pieces, and next best to these, the brisket and rounds.

Rebecca Jackson's Rice Pudding.

Take 1 quart of rich milk; $\frac{3}{4}$ of a coffee-cup of rice, well washed, and a lump of butter the size of an egg, and 1 nutmeg. This pudding must be made quite sweet, and without eggs. Bake three hours in a moderate oven, stirring occasionally the first hour. Bake until the top is a dark brown. To be eaten cold.

[This pudding—which was a common dish in the last century—was generally baked on Saturday for Sunday's dessert.]

Bread-and-Butter Pudding.

To 1 quart of milk, add 3 or 4 eggs, well beaten, with sugar enough to make rather sweet, and season with nutmeg or cinnamon. Put in a baking-pan and cover with slices of nice bread, buttered on both sides. Bake until the bread is nicely browned, taking care, however, not to bake too much, which would make it watery. Good either hot or cold.

Codfish Cakes.

Pick boiled codfish in small bits, adding equal quantities of mashed potato and fish, with two eggs, well beaten, seasoning with black pepper, and roll in a little flour, the shape of a small cake. Fry in sweet lard, or nice drippings, to a nice brown, but not hard.

Pickled Grapes.

Remove from ripe grapes all imperfect and broken berries; line an earthen jar with grape leaves and fill with grapes. To 2 quarts vinegar add 1 pint white sugar, ½ ounce ground cinnamon, and ¼ ounce cloves. Let vinegar and spices boil five minutes; then add the sugar, and, when moderately cool, pour over the grapes.

FORCED TOMATOES.

Peel and slice some large-sized tomatoes, and put in a colander to drain. Cut in small pieces 1 pint of mushrooms, adding some minced parsley, a slice of finely chopped ham, some summer savory, thyme, salt, and cayenne pepper. Put all these in a saucepan with some butter, and ½ cup of water. Boil together ten or fifteen minutes, and set away to cool. Have ready some fine bread crumbs, add to them seasoning, and the yolks of 2 or 3 well-beaten eggs. Mix the mushrooms and tomatoes together; pour into a baking-dish a portion of it; then sprinkle over it a layer of the bread-crumbs and add the remainder of the tomatoes; cover with bread-crumbs, and put some bits of butter on top. Bake half-an-hour in a well heated oven.

BROILED FLOUNDERS OR SMELTS.

Have medium-sized flounders or smelts, cleaned with as little cutting as possible; wash thoroughly in salted water, and dry on a towel; mix in a saucer three tablespoonfuls of olive oil, and 1 of vinegar, with salt and pepper; score the sides of the fish at intervals of an inch, with a sharp knife, and rub all over with the mixture of oil, vinegar and seasoning. Place them between the bars of a buttered gridiron, and broil a light brown over a moderate fire.

ONIONS.

There is no more healthy vegetable or article of diet in general use than onions. Taken regularly, they greatly promote the health of the lungs and digestive organs. Used in a cooked—either fried, roasted or boiled—or in a raw state, their virtues are marked and beneficial. They are among the most popular of old-time remedies for colds, having the advantage of always being readily procured, and it is said that affections of the lungs and liver have been largely benefited, and even cured, by a free use of this palatable esculent. They are also resorted to as a sedative and remedy for sleeplessness.

Singeing Fowls.

The best mode I have ever followed for singeing fowls, is to put 2 or 3 tablespoonfuls of alcohol in a tin dish and light with a match, thus making a large flame, without smoke—that is apt to injure the flavor of the bird.

The Secret of Tests of Taste and Flavor.

The correct test of coffee or tea, is to make use of a thin china or delf-ware cup, by which the lips are brought close together, while a thicker cup would separate them widely apart. In testing the quality and flavor of wines, the thinnest quality of glass is for the same reason essentially requisite. Our grandmothers, who lived a hundred years ago, understood the philosophy of this when they expressed the opinion, that it was only possible to get the true taste, fine flavor, and delicate aroma of tea, by drinking it out of a china cup.

How to Choose Ware for Ranges.

In selecting ware for a range, especial care should be taken to see that the bottoms of all the cooking utensils are perfectly level, for if convex, they will invariably burn in the centre. An iron grating or gridiron—$\frac{1}{4}$ of an inch in depth—placed between the pan and the top of the range, will be found highly useful while cooking, as this increases the heat and lessens the liability of burning.

Drying Herbs for Seasoning.

All herbs should be gathered just before blossoming and dried in the shade, or in a dark dry room, as exposure to the sun both takes away flavor and color. When perfectly dry, put in a clean sack and hang in a dry room or loft, and when wanted for use, rub through a sieve. Herbs treated in this way, if left dry, will retain their strength and remain perfectly good for years. As long as the outer membrane of the leaves remains unbroken, the aroma cannot escape.

To Destroy Roaches, Flies and Ants.

Take 15 cents worth of powdered borax and a small bottle of Persian Insect Powder, and mix thoroughly together. In order to use successfully, take a feather from the wing of a turkey or goose, by the quill, and dipping the feather end in the powder, spring the feather as a bow; in this way you can thoroughly rid the room of flies. Before using on roaches, set the doors wide open, as they will start for the open air; generally, however, dying on the way. To rid cupboards or closets of ants, sprinkle wherever these minute pests "most do congregate." An easy and cheap remedy to rid pantries of cock-roaches is said to be fresh cucumber parings laid in their haunts. We have never tested this remedy, but can vouch for the efficacy of the above mentioned compound.

To Clean Tin-Ware.

The best thing for cleaning tin-ware is common soda; dampen a cloth, dip it in the soda, rub the ware briskly, after which wipe dry.

Iron Rust.

Iron rust may be removed by a little salt mixed with lemon-juice; put in the sun, and if necessary use two applications.

Mildew.

An old time and effectual remedy for mildew is to dip the stained cloth in butter-milk and lay in the sun.

Oysters Roasted on Chafing-Dish.

Take largest oysters, and put in a chafing-dish in their own liquor. Season with red or black pepper, adding plenty of good butter, with a little

Worcestershire sauce or walnut catsup. After roasting—taking care not to roast too much—serve on buttered toast.

Codfish, Family Style.

After the fish has been soaked twelve hours, boil slowly for twenty-five or thirty minutes, or until it will break up nicely. Then pick all the bones out, but do not pick the fish too fine. Have ready three hard-boiled eggs; rub the yolks in plenty of good butter; put into the kettle enough milk to heat the fish; when hot stir in the butter, with the fish. At the same time have potatoes peeled and boiled. Cut, not too small, with the whites of the eggs cut small; season with pepper. Serve hot with buttered toast at the bottom of the dish.

Codfish in Philadelphia Style.

After soaking and boiling the fish, break up small, and picking out all the bones, have ready potatoes, peeled and boiled, equal to the amount of fish. Put them in a wooden bowl or tray. Pound or mash well with a potato masher. Work to soft dough, with butter and well-beaten eggs, and milk or cream. Season with pepper and salt, if salt is required. Put it in a dish suitable to set on the table, and bake a few minutes, or until light brown.

www.ingramcontent.com/pod-product-compliance
Lightning Source LLC
Chambersburg PA
CBHW081125080526
44587CB00021B/3748